DO YOU
MIND
IF I
CANCEL?

DO YOU MIND IF I CANCEL?

(Things That Still Annoy Me)

GARY JANETTI

FLATIRON
BOOKS
NEW YORK

DO YOU MIND IF I CANCEL? Copyright © 2019 by Gary Janetti. All rights reserved. Printed in the United States of America. For information, address Flatiron Books, 120 Broadway, New York, NY 10271.

www.flatironbooks.com

Library of Congress Cataloging-in-Publication Data

Names: Janetti, Gary, 1966– author.
Title: Do you mind if I cancel? : (things that still annoy me) / Gary Janetti.
Description: First U.S. edition. | New York : Flatiron Books, 2019.
Identifiers: LCCN 2019031743 | ISBN 9781250225825 (hardcover) | ISBN 9781250266415 (international, sold outside the U.S., subject to rights availability) | ISBN 9781250225849 (ebook)
Subjects: LCSH: Janetti, Gary, 1966– —Anecdotes. | Television producers and directors—United States—Biography.
Classification: LCC PN1992.4.J36 A3 2019 | DDC 791.4502/3092 [B]—dc23
LC record available at https://lccn.loc.gov/2019031743

Our books may be purchased in bulk for promotional, educational, or business use. Please contact your local bookseller or the Macmillan Corporate and Premium Sales Department at 1-800-221-7945, extension 5442, or by email at MacmillanSpecialMarkets@macmillan.com.

First U.S. Edition: October 2019
First International Edition: October 2019

10   9   8   7   6   5   4   3   2   1

For Brad

and for

Mom and Dad

CONTENTS

DO YOU
MIND
IF I
CANCEL?

LEND-A-HAND

I'm twenty-four or twenty-five. What does it matter? Twentysomething. It's all just one age, really. I thought there was a difference at the time. I remember graduating college at twenty-two and wanting to join the Peace Corps, but when I found out the commitment was two years, I reacted like it was a block of time I could barely comprehend. "Two years?! But I'll be twenty-*four* when it's over!"

I only really wanted to join because I liked to travel and be around attractive people. The helping others aspect of it was not at the forefront of my mind. It was mostly me, incredibly lean and tan, sipping a drink at some local rooftop bar in an exotic city somewhere like Marrakech or Istanbul surrounded by young, handsome selfless men such as myself. The actual mechanics of the Peace Corps never entered into it. It was more about the going out after work part and the weekend trips to remote beaches with simple chic lodgings for five U.S. dollars a night.

During my imaginary stint in the Peace Corps I would grow my hair out. The climate and water in my new country would do wonders for it, making it more full-bodied and manageable than it ever was in New York. I wouldn't fuss with it though. I would be too busy helping people dig a well or teaching them something that would no doubt improve their lives. Whenever I would get complimented on it, which would be often, I would tell people it's only this long for practical reasons. "I can tuck it behind my ears and I won't have to bother with it." Even though a perfect lock would flop over an eye every time I bent down to lift another shovelful of dirt, forcing me to exhale exasperatedly to blow it out of my face because I couldn't possibly be bothered tucking it behind my ear *again*.

Due to all the physical labor I was performing my body would transform itself into something out of a magazine practically overnight. I would not notice it though. Too consumed with my work in the village to be bothered by such trivial matters. Although it would be hard for me to avoid with the constant attention it would embarrassingly bring me. The girls in the village giggling shyly when I crossed the dirt square that served as the community's central gathering place with a long stick across my bulging shoulders straining to hold the enormous buckets of water at either end. I would smile at them and call out their names as I passed, pronouncing each unique one perfectly.

I would be beloved in the village. And I would become best friends with the volunteer who worked in the next village over. So close I could walk there at the end of the day so we could enjoy a beer together, bonding over our shared passion for helping those in need. Josh would be blond. And have a deep voice. And we would be exactly one month apart in age. And he would've been a champion swimmer in college who was on an Olympic track but had to put his dreams aside when a knee injury forced him to rethink his life. We would talk about this constantly. Me being the reassuring friend. His entire support system. His confidant each night as he breaks down in my arms. "Who am I if I can't swim?" "It's okay, Josh, shh, I'm here."

And then I would get sick. Or Josh would get sick. One of us would get sick. Probably him. And during this time we would profess our love for each other. And one would nurse the other back to health.

And our affair would be lit like a *National Geographic* special. Yellow sunrises, golden sunsets, clear starlit skies.

It's about this time that the villagers and any kind of charitable work pretty much disappear from my imaginary time in the Peace Corps.

This part on is mostly beaches and tanning. A photo spread of young love as envisioned by *Condé Nast Traveler*.

But the thought of being gone for an entire two years is enough to dissuade me from this potential new life. The fact that what I was actually looking for was an extended warm-weather vacation with a fitness model as opposed to the life-altering growth experience that the Peace Corps in reality was never enters into the equation. I decide not to apply. I would be too old by the time I returned. It would be too late to start my career as a novelist, which I have just decided I want to be. I would lose too much time. I would miss too much.

Two years go by in about a second and I accomplish absolutely nothing. Literally thinking on my twenty-fourth birthday, Shit, I should've joined the Peace Corps I wouldn't have missed a thing.

Well, I would've missed being a cashier, and an office temp and a salesman at Ralph Lauren but that's it. I still have plans on becoming a novelist even though I have no idea what that entails. Aside from writing. Which I haven't done yet. Better to get life experience first. I can't write about nothing.

To that end I take a new job. It's for an agency called Lend-A-Hand. Lend-A-Hand matches people looking for someone to do a job for them, any job, with the people who are desperate enough to do them.

This was an awful time in the world, just before the internet, when you actually had to go into places in person to meet with prospective employers. Requiring you to speak with varying assistants and assorted others many steps along the way.

I'm not one of those people who goes on about how much

better things used to be before the horrors of social media and modern technology. On the contrary, I wish there were more of it. I wish there were a way to slash at least another 50 percent of all human interaction. Nobody has that much to say when you get right down to it. I prefer a life of texting and scrolling Instagram to one of having to pick up the phone and talk to someone like an animal. No, thank you. You can keep your nostalgia. I wish to God I were a millennial. I'd be so good at it. Better than these shitty ones. I wouldn't be wasting my time being offended by every little thing or promoting positive body images or getting involved in politics. I'd be avoiding people. I'd be working from home. I'd be watching TV on my laptop. They don't know the nightmare it was to actually have had to talk to people *all* the time. And we weren't allowed to have social anxiety like you are now. Nobody even knew about it. I would have been in heaven if I could have suffered from anxiety.

But here I am, in my twenties, with no technology, having to make an appointment on the phone and I don't know who I'm going to talk to because I can't Google anyone and since I don't even know what that is at the time I don't miss it but knowing now what it is and thinking back on how different it was then I feel like I came of age in pioneer times and it's not fair. So, no, I don't care if everyone is looking at their fucking phone now. They should be. It tells you everything.

Does any of this matter when I'm twenty-four or twenty-five and going into Lend-A-Hand for an interview? It doesn't.

But it annoys me when I think of how much easier everything could've been.

The Lend-A-Hand office is small and cluttered and there is one woman who works there. She sits behind a desk with a stack of index cards on them. Each card has an available job on it. They range from cleaning apartments to cater waiter for a private party—the most sought-after job she tells me, often involving large tips and the glamour that's associated with serving cocktails to people who can afford to hire help.

Getting into a wealthy person's Upper East Side apartment is the perfect gateway to my career as a successful author I decide. Or even an actor. Who's to say at this point, and really I shouldn't limit myself. It's quite possible that I could find myself serving flutes of champagne to gallery owners and opera patrons when someone approaches me and says "excuse me, have you ever acted?" I'll look around modestly to make sure they are indeed talking to me. "Me?" "Yes, you." "A little. In college, but . . ." Let them know you *have* done some acting, you're not a complete rube, but also that you don't really care tremendously one way or the other. This will make you even that much more appealing. "Here's my card." (People had cards then, it was the one delightful touch that I miss.) "Call me. We may have something for you on *All My Children*." And just like that I'd be starring on a soap opera. (*All My Children* is long off the air, but then, in the '90s, a person would die to be on it. I had a professor in college who taught a class on scene work. He was an adjunct professor, which basically means any idiot off the street, but at the time I didn't know that. This adjunct professor had the distinction of appearing in a handful of episodes of *All My Children* as the bartender in Pine Valley's most elegant restaurant, The Chateau. And I swear it was as if Laurence fucking Olivier were teaching that class. A cast member from *All My Children*. Here, on Long Island. At Hofstra University. I was really in the thick of it.)

Now starring on a soap opera had never been part of the plan. But if this producer saw something special in me that I didn't see myself, well then who was I to argue? This is how careers are born. You put yourself in front of the right people and then step aside. Anything could happen.

And besides, all the jobs I did for Lend-A-Hand I could just chalk up as research for my novel, which I was determined to start at some point. When the time was right. So in essence *I* wouldn't really be bartending or helping someone move or mopping floors but rather researching what it would be like to *be* someone who did those things.

Unfortunately in order to get the good Lend-A-Hand assignments you had to prove yourself by taking any available ones offered to you. This is what I am told by the woman in charge of handing out jobs. I, of course, say I would be willing to take on any job, which is how I find myself less than twenty-four hours later cleaning the bathroom of an NYU linguistics professor as his family sits in the living room pretending I'm not there. Later, while I'm on my knees scrubbing this family's disgusting toilet (who by the way all look perfectly capable of scrubbing their own fucking toilet) I think, "I have a degree I have potential I have dreams, how did I end up someone who cleans apartments?" Then I remind myself *I'm* not someone who cleans apartments, I'm only researching what it's like to *be* someone who cleans apartments, and feel much better.

When I try to decline the next cleaning assignment offered to me and hold out instead for one of the plummier catering gigs I'm told by the woman on the phone (today this would all thank God be done with an app) that if I don't take this job she can't promise I'll ever rise to the ranks of Upper East Side cater waiter. Seeing as this is the one stumbling block to my contract role on *All My Children* I accept the offer to clean the apartment of a disabled, gay octogenarian on Gramercy Park.

And I can already see how it's going to play out. I'll show up and he'll immediately be so enamored of my good looks (*and* how unaware of them I seem to be—only making me that much more attractive) and my charming conversational skills that in no time at all we'll be flipping through old *Playbill*s from shows starring Ethel Merman and Mary Martin, sipping cognac (or whatever it is eighty-year-old, disabled, gay men drink) and talking about our love of musical theater. When I finally say something like "Well, I should get started . . . ," he stops me, "Please, you're not cleaning anything. You should be in a magazine not cleaning apartments." Then I look down with great humility and say something like "Hey, a job's a job," and before I can utter another word he presses two crisp hundred-dollar bills into my palm and shows me to the door. "Thank you for bringing life back into my home. Tomorrow? Same time?" "I'd like that," I say in the kind of tone that implies I may have gotten more out of the afternoon than he did. And before you know it I'm in the will and that Gramercy Park apartment is mine. Stranger things have happened. And I'd be a fool not to explore every opportunity open to me. Besides, what a great chapter in my novel this will make!

When I arrive at the address, however, and the old gay wheels himself down the hallway shouting orders at me it becomes all too quickly clear that I'm actually going to have to clean this fucking pigsty. My cute outfit now seems impractical considering I hadn't dressed to do anything other than leaf through Broadway memorabilia and look angelic. As he points me to the trash bags and disinfectant I'll need for defrosting his refrigerator and freezer I have to admit to myself that the odds of inheriting this place are not looking good.

After hours of being barked at with a laundry list of increasingly labor-intensive, anally compulsive chores I begin to wonder if this guy is even gay. I've deliberately dusted all the highest shelves first in order to afford him a glimpse of my midriff, but not even a glance. At this point I'd be willing to take a shower in front of him if it meant I didn't have to clean it. Instead he yells at me from the kitchen because I didn't arrange all the canned goods according to size and color. It's actually offensive. We're sixty years apart in age for fuck's sake I should be driving him insane, this should be *Death in Venice* not *Oliver Twist*! I've just about reached the end of my rope when I notice something peeking out from an overstuffed drawer. A *Playbill* from *Gypsy* starring Ethel Merman. And I throw it out.

The ride home on the subway is crowded. And I pretend Josh is there, leaning up against me, so close, his breath on my face. We carry bags of groceries and plan to stay in and cook that night, like we do most nights. Later, as I lay in his arms, I tell him "I'm scared."

PATTI LUPONE

⁓

I grow up in Queens in the '70s. During this period there are tons of commercials for Broadway shows. I become obsessed, studying each one with the concentrated focus of a brain surgeon. But the commercial I was most fixated on was for *Evita* starring Patti LuPone. Every time it came on it was like a jolt of cocaine coursed through my twelve-year-old body. "What's new, Buenos Aires?" she sang. What *was* new, Buenos Aires? I was desperate to find out. And then of course "Don't Cry for Me Argentina," her arms open wide. Mandy Patinkin is in it, too, but he's clearly no match for Patti. When I die I hope this commercial is the last thing that flashes through my mind. I'd never heard of Patti before *Evita*, but it was like she had always existed.

I buy the original cast recording and listen to it for hours.

I learn every word. I am Eva, I am Che, I am Juan Perón, I am even the mistress who gets thrown out into the street (whose one song, "Another Suitcase in Another Hall," Madonna steals for herself in the movie, telling you pretty much everything you need to know about Madonna).

Several times a year, once we've saved enough money, my parents let my sister Maria and me go into the city to see a Broadway matinee. We take the express bus into Manhattan for a 2:00 P.M. Wednesday performance of *Evita*. I don't have a child but I can't imagine the excitement on the day of its birth could come anything near to what I feel that afternoon. The soundtrack buzzing through me like a drug. I haven't eaten in days, my stomach too unsettled with anticipation. "I'm coming, Patti." I downplay all of this to my sister, of course. We're both very excited, don't get me wrong. But she is excited in the way in which a sane person would be, saying things like "I can't wait." Meanwhile I'm thinking, "Can't wait?? That doesn't even begin to cut it!" I'm undone, every nerve ending vibrating, I haven't been able to concentrate on another thought since we got the tickets over a month ago—if my heart were beating any faster I'd have a stroke!

"I can't wait either," I say.

We go to Bun and Brew for lunch. Dark and filled with theatergoers and business people, it's all too impossibly sophisticated. Of course this is actually a shithole but I don't know that because I'm twelve. The burger goes down like a fistful of sand, so anxious am I about the show you'd think I was starring in it. "I'm almost there, Patti."

We arrive at the theater thirty minutes early. Panicked at the thought of having to go to the bathroom during the show I force myself to pee so many times it looks like I'm cruising the men's room. We are shown by the usher to our seats in the orchestra and handed our programs. Off to the side but not bad. The musicians filing into the pit, the remaining theatergoers being seated, so pumped am I with adrenaline right now that I could lift a car. In the minutes before the show starts I quickly open my *Playbill* to read Patti's bio when a small slip of paper falls out onto my lap:

Today's matinee will be performed by Nancy Opel.

What?! I shove the paper in my sister's face. "Did you fucking see this?!" Maria says something like, "I'm sure she's just as good." "JUST AS GOOD AS PATTI?? THAT'S NOT POSSIBLE!!" I have never felt such rage in my life before and all of it is directed at Nancy Opel. I *hate* Nancy Opel. The orchestra begins to play. This can't be happening. I sit with my arms crossed. Every fiber of my being devoted to letting Nancy Opel know just how much I loathe and despise her. (Today you would go online and you would know exactly which performances someone was or wasn't in or they would announce it on Twitter or Instagram and something as horrific as this would have been avoided. I couldn't afford to see *Evita* again nor would the thought ever have even occurred to me—this was it. *Evita* starring Nancy Opel *not* Patti LuPone. What cruel joke of the universe was this?)

From the second the show began it was apparent this was not going to sound like the original cast album that was playing in my head. Let me make one thing clear right now, Nancy Opel is not Patti LuPone. (Years later I see Nancy Opel in another show where she is brilliant but I can't help myself from thinking "you're still not Patti.") She didn't look like her, she didn't sound like her, and I was having none of it. Sitting there with my arms crossed, completely unimpressed. "What's new, Buenos Aires?" she sang. I didn't give a fuck. At the end of each number I would listlessly clap. Yawning every time she opened her mouth to sing just to let her know that I was on to her. At intermission I became the jaded theatergoer. Yes, I was enjoying the show. The sets, the costumes, all marvelous. Yes, Mandy Patinkin is splendid. But don't you think the girl playing Evita is a little too, well, not Patti? At the start of act two when it was time for her to sing "Don't Cry for Me Argentina" it was all I could do to keep from jumping onto my seat screaming "IMPOSTER!"

"She was good," my sister says later when we're walking back to the bus stop. "Uh-huh," I say, barely able to muster the enthusiasm to speak "she was *fine*."

Now when the commercial for *Evita* would come on it was like a kick in the stomach. "Why wasn't Nancy Opel in the commercial if she was so fucking good, huh, Maria?!"

Evita runs for several more years and the commercial with

Patti continues to play even after she is long gone from the show. But I feel nothing now.

It's not that I believe that Patti and I are fighting, that would be insane. But something is broken between us.

When I am nineteen I attend a summer acting program at Oxford University. It's not actually affiliated with Oxford, the courses are just being held there, but it sounds suitably exclusive at the time. *Brideshead Revisited* but with a Queens accent. This is literally months before I come out (my hand already slowly turning the closet doorknob), and considering the entire male population of England also seems to exist in that limbo state somewhere between straight and gay it's the perfect place to pass my final weeks of nonspecific sexuality.

The teachers are mostly members of The Acting Company, a theater group founded by long-dead actor John Houseman. In order to avoid any awkward questions, I have outfitted myself with an imaginary girlfriend who lives in Bermuda (I don't know why). So sad to think I wasted my nineteen-year-old beauty that summer on a nonexistent girl who I didn't even bother to give a name instead of meeting some pale, doe-eyed, flopsy-haired Brit. I drop the ruse halfway through the program (so little caring is left in me at this point) saying something like "oh, yeah, no, I ended things with . . . her." I sound quite callous, which I like. At this point I think if a man even brushed up against me I would've exploded out of the closet,

so ready was I to move into a phase of my life that didn't in-
volve bottling up every emotion until it led to crippling head-
aches. But that didn't happen. What did happen was that one
of our teachers had a friend in London who was rehearsing
a new musical and she would be coming by one day to teach
us a class. And this person just happened to be Patti fucking
LuPone. How is anybody even friends with Patti LuPone, I
wondered. But this teacher was. And I told him how much I
wanted to meet her and what she meant to me (just basics, not
enough to scare him), and he said that he'd tell her and that he
was sure she would be happy to meet me. This was all too much
to process. "So . . . here we are again, Patti."

(One of my classmates at "not really Oxford" is David
Schwimmer, who would go on to star in *Friends*. We are very
friendly that summer and hang out with the same general
group of people, which is pretty hard *not* to do considering
there were only about twenty or so of us in the program. I remember David taking his "craft" very seriously at eighteen, so
I wasn't surprised when later he became famous. I mention
this because ten years after we graduate from this program
and I have just started writing for TV in Los Angeles I go to
a *Friends* taping and after the show I'm brought down to the
set by a coworker where I see David. Now at this time I'm new
to Hollywood and dealing with celebrity, so I mistakenly treat
David as I would any other person I had been friends with ten
years previously. I say hello. He looks at me confused. Could
I possibly be talking to him? "It's me . . . Gary . . . from Ox-

ford." Still he looks around. I start to feel dread. "We took an acting program together for two months, remember?" And then I begin to list all the things that happened that summer that might jog his memory. Still nothing. Now I'm completely unhinged. Did I even go to Oxford? Was I ever even nineteen?? "I'm sorry, that was such a long time ago," he says. Then he holds his hand out and introduces himself to me, "I'm David." Yeah, I know who the fuck you are. I didn't realize at the time that I was in the rearview mirror of his fame and he was not looking back. Or maybe his past didn't exist anymore, whereas mine only became crisper, clearer, moments playing back like scenes from a favorite TV show. He is part of my memory even still. Even now. And when members of the Royal Shakespeare Company come to teach a master class at the end of the program and several of us are chosen to perform scenes, I can still see David and his scene partner performing just before I am chosen to perform next with my scene partner. And I can still remember the feeling I had when I did well. I can still feel the smile on my face. I remember being nervous to follow him because he was so good. I remember us all eating in the dining hall and going to the National Theatre to see Ian McKellen in *Coriolanus* and I remember us drinking beer at the picnic tables along the Thames before the show and I re- member him coming with me to buy a suit in London because I was going to be returning to New York on the *QE2* because my dad worked for Cunard Line and I found out I could go for free (but I couldn't afford a suit and my roommate, another

David, so kind, lends me his) and I remember he wore eye-liner because it was the '8os and he was punk and I remember his denim jacket lined with fleece and I remember talking and taking pictures and sitting on the grass. I remembered it all. And he remembered none of it. Well, not *me* anyway. But isn't that always the risk you take when you say to someone, "remember?")

I wait excitedly for the day when Patti will come. I can't help but feel there is some unfinished business between us but I decide I won't mention this. Or maybe I will. Maybe Patti and I will get along like a house on fire and she will instantly see my full potential. "Who is this kid? He's got something really special!" And she will invite me to coffee or dinner and when I reluctantly (not really) tell her about not seeing her in *Evita* and how devastated I was she will be charmed and we will laugh. And it will have all been worth it because it would have brought us to this moment. Life is funny like that, I've heard people say. And I wanted to say it, too.

But she doesn't ever come. Patti. She is rehearsing for a role in a new musical we're told. (This musical is *Les Misérables*. I know.) She is sorry to have to cancel. Or so says my acting teacher. This young man. Who doesn't seem young to me then but really must have been only a few years older than the rest of us. And he tells me he mentioned to her that there was a student very much looking forward to meeting her (as he told me he would) and she tells him to tell me how sad she is to have to miss me. And it's fucking Nancy Opel all over again.

And the program ends and I sail back alone on the *QE2* to New York (which I don't think is weird at the time but it is, very). And I wear the suit my roommate David (not David Schwimmer) lends me to dinner for formal nights on the ship. (And I bump into him again many years later, this roommate, long after I have mailed the suit back, when he, too, has become a successful actor and he remembers me and I him.) And I go back to college and I come out and I meet a boy and I graduate and years later I go to Greece and meet another boy, who will become my husband, and on the night we meet we talk until morning. And he tells me about seeing Patti LuPone sing "I Dreamed a Dream" from *Les Miz* on TV in Canada. And I think, I could fall in love with this person. And I do. And and and and and so many ands later and here I am.

Oh, but to see that commercial. Evita's arms outstretched, proud, defiant. It was like a door had opened and Patti was welcoming me. "Come in," she said. "Come in."

PARAMOUNT

I'm twenty-six years old. I quit my previous job working as the receptionist for a nonprofit educational theater company at NYU (at least I think I quit, somebody might have implied—said—maybe it's time you move on Gary) before I have another job in place. This is the first time I have ever left a job before I already have the next one lined up. I estimate I can survive on my savings for two days, three if I just sit in a corner.

I had always marveled at people who quit their job before they had their next one and said things like "I might travel for a while, go to Thailand for a month." How did these people live?? What were they traveling on?? But I just assumed this was one more of those things that I didn't know about (like the Hamptons. I was born in Queens, spent my summers going to Jones Beach on Long Island, and never once heard anyone say the word Hamptons until I was twenty-one. When I finally go there, several years later, I can't believe that this paradise had been only two hours away from me my entire life. Now everyone knows about the Hamptons, it's as gross as everywhere else. But then, going for the first time, I was almost embarrassed that it had been so close all this while and I was completely unaware. Stepping foot there I felt like Dorothy in Oz, only instead of encountering Munchkins it was rich cunts.) Every cent of every paycheck was instantly accounted for the second I got it (my salary was just enough to pay my bills and sink me incrementally just a little further into debt). As soon as one check stopped the entire operation would fall apart.

I answer an ad in *The Village Voice* (the *Village Voice* was the internet in the '90s) for an open call to work at the Paramount Hotel. I'm curious as to why there is a cattle call audition to work in a hotel until I discover that the new owner of this hotel is Ian Schrager of Studio 54 fame, fresh out of prison for tax evasion. It is the '90s and hotels are the new discos he has decreed. I've never thought of working in a hotel but I enjoy *staying* in a hotel, so how different could it be? Besides at this point I've been out of work for a week. (I tried to find something before leaving my job at NYU but I discovered I didn't have any skills other than working in the service indus-try. I'm planning on being a novelist, yes, but that apparently doesn't amount to a skill. Especially when you haven't written anything yet. And asking people to take your word that you're a writer in an interview doesn't open as many doors as I had hoped it would.)

I show up at the Roseland Ballroom (site of the first circuit parties, but now, like most places I danced in my twenties, a luxury apartment building) for the "interview," which appears to have attracted every person under thirty in New York. If this many people are out of a job, who's actually working? It is a dehumanizing experience where the first step is a cursory glance of your looks that results in either moving to the next step or going home. I'm, thank fucking God, directed to the next step (my entire self-worth now hinging on two middle-aged women with clipboards and one vicious gay man), which basically involves a closer scrutiny of your looks and some slight speaking. (This was during a simpler time when you could hire and fire someone based on looks, weight, age, and no one would so much as bat an eye). A few hours later and I'm still there and our numbers have dwindled down to about a dozen and I'm having my final interview. At this point I'm so desperate to be selected I'd let them strip me naked and put me on a revolving turntable until I remember that what I'm competing for is not a modeling contract or a part in a major motion picture but the chance to work behind the front desk of a midtown hotel.

I get the job. So much humiliation for so little (yet still the tiny voice shouts "they picked me!").

The hotel is from the early 1900s but is newly designed by

Philippe Starck and looks like the interior of an ocean liner crossed with a sex dungeon. I am surrounded by attractive men and women all in their mid-twenties. If someone over thirty is employed here I haven't seen them. And since nobody who works at this hotel is actually interested in a career in the hospitality industry (they are models or actors, all good-looking people are secretly hoping to cash in on their looks by doing the least amount possible), it's not particularly service-oriented. I'm given maybe an hour of training and then thrown behind the front desk and told to ask Tammy, the clerk who works beside me, if I have any questions. I try to figure out the computer (which is huge and unnecessarily complicated and much harder to use than anything that exists today, everything was awful then) as people check in and out. Whenever I ask Tammy a question she ignores me, too busy herself trying to figure this shit out having just started the week before me. When I persist she snaps, "I can't help you!" (Attractive people and gay people get overwhelmed quite easily. I once saw a beautiful gay salesman almost quit his job at Barneys when a second person joined the line. It all became too much for him. And I totally understood. I rolled my eyes for the both of us.)

The bellmen at the hotel stand at attention in the center of the lobby. When it is time to show a guest to their room we are told to ring the bell and the bellman whose turn it is will then approach and we say something like "James, will you show Mr. and Mrs. Smith to room 502?"

I ring the bell and Tom, a tall humorless bellman, approaches. Tom, will you show, etc. He seems annoyed with me for some unknown reason but takes the guests to their room. Immediately after he walks up to the desk.

"That was really disrespectful."

"What was?"

"I don't like answering to a bell."

"But . . . you're a bellman."

"Just don't do it again."

"Oh, you didn't ring the bell for Tom, did you?" someone asks me. "I did because he's the bellman." "Yeah, when it's Tom just shout across the lobby 'Tom!' and he'll come. The other bellmen don't mind the bell, though." Which is good news I guess considering their choice of occupation.

After a few extraordinarily stressful weeks I get the hang of it and am only too happy when someone else new starts and asks me a question and I get to respond "I'm really busy right now I can only do ten things at once I'll be with you in a second okay JESUS!"

Working at the hotel is already giving me a lot of fodder for my novel, I decide. Too much to keep track of even. I intend to start carrying a little notebook around with me to write down all my thoughts and ideas. And then basically type that up and there you go. Book. But for the time being I'm too busy working eight hours a day and growing my hair out. (All guys have long hair in the early '90s, if you can't tuck your hair behind your ears you might as well not exist.)

Sometimes when you work back-to-back shifts (3:00 P.M.

to 11:00 P.M., and then 7:00 A.M. to 3:00 P.M., ingrained into my brain for eternity), they let you sleep in an empty room and I imagine myself a successful writer on a book tour or an actor filming on location and for those brief hours my life is full and I'm successful and everything is just as it should be.

Months later I become obsessed with one of the bellmen. Jason. He is straight and perfect. His face, hair, body. He is a model (part-time catalogue work so impressive to me I can barely form the words "you've been in a magazine?" How does a person even get in a magazine?? These must be the same people who travel to Southeast Asia for a month between jobs) and bright and personable and a bit odd. I imagine he needs a kidney and I am an exact match and I donate mine to him and this connects us for life. He tells me he's never had a brother. Until now.

Of course there is, in the back of my mind, like a constant white noise, the hum of "maybe he's gay, maybe he's gay, maybe he's gay." I ignore the hum, it gets fainter over time, but never goes away completely. When I see him in the locker room with his shirt off I almost faint so sculpted is his body. Not a blemish, bump, or hair. Every inch defined. It should be in medical journals. Scientists should study him. I feel oily and misshapen in comparison. Not fit to breathe Jason's air. I turn away (it's almost too much to look at) using all of my self-control not to simply reach out and touch his skin.

Around this time I realize that the bellmen make more money than the front desk clerks, and I want in on it. I also realize that all of the gay guys work behind the front desk and the straight guys work as bellmen. I'm not fucking having it, and I become Norma Gay (this is a pun based on the film *Norma Rae*, starring Sally Field as a worker who forms a union, she won an Oscar, you really should know this) and insist that I be given the same opportunity to carry people's luggage and grovel for tips as my straight attractive brothers. I get the job and move over from the front desk to join the ranks of the bellmen. What I now know was a lateral career move at the time seemed like a major victory.

As a new bellman my shift is 11:00 P.M. to 7:00 A.M. Also on the overnight shift due to his busy modeling schedule (could you die?) is Jason.

A few nights a week, when it's very late and not busy, we hang out in the basement of the hotel (which decades ago used to be a nightclub but is now a crumbling, ghostlike ruin—and soooooo romantic) and have deep talks about whatever topic Jason was into that day. I let him steer the conversations, dissecting every word for a hidden message that never comes. Jason gets stoned. I do occasionally but only to be polite. So afraid am I of doing anything to upset our budding friendship. We're a tiny club of two. And at 3:00 A.M., when I can barely keep my eyes open, just a smile from him hits me like a pot of coffee and I'm wide awake the rest of the night. This goes on for weeks, months. And then I don't remember what happens or when it happens or why it happens but I get bored, I guess, I think, and we stop hanging out together and I start working different shifts and then he eventually leaves (goes back to school, stops modeling, something like that) and I have other friends at the hotel and I'm dating a guy and then another guy and then I just forget. The way you do. (I guess, I think. I see him once after this on a plane a few years later and he's still handsome but thin, the body not what it was I can't help noticing, and we talk and it's strange and also lovely. And then, not long ago, I think of him. I don't know why. Maybe because I'm older and that's what happens. I wonder what he looks like now. What he's doing. Who he is. And I look for him online and find out he died. Jason. And I see us clearly in the basement of the hotel. Black, shiny hair. His perfect smile. And we're both young. I don't think I ever even hugged him.)

I work at the hotel longer than I intend. I get free theater tickets, and I get into clubs, and I've finally grown my hair out. I am a part of everything and nothing.

I'm in the lobby talking to the other bellman on duty when I recognize someone checking in. A friend I haven't seen since college. He is here on a business trip. And the bell rings. And I am called to the desk. "Gary, this is Mr. Carp, he's checking into room 801." (And in this moment I understand how Tom felt about answering to a bell.) He immediately recognizes me, this old friend. Is happy to see me. He feels weird about me carrying his luggage but I insist, make a joke of it. Pretending I don't mind and am glad to have this time to catch up, and when we get to his room he reaches into his pocket to give me a tip and I feel my stomach turn over and I say "no, please, it's okay." He tries to insist. "I said it's okay" and he can hear the anger in my voice. We stand there for a moment. Stuck, it feels like, forever. Then plan to get together but know we never will.

Because I'm working back-to-back shifts I spend the night in the hotel. Only the longer I work there the harder it is imagining myself a successful writer on a book tour or an actor filming on location or anything else that I'm not.

And then I wake up and I'm alone in a hotel room I could never afford in debt about to get back into the uniform I wore the night before and I have to plaster a smile on my face and I have no prospects, no career, no skills, and suddenly I'm twenty-eight. And I feel sick. And I still have no little notebook to write any of this down in.

THE WILLIAM ESPER STUDIO

While I'm in graduate school at NYU I work as a resident assistant in the Carlyle student dorms. Thankfully this is before cell phones or the internet so you could disappear for pretty much days on end without anyone thinking too much of it. I spent many of my nights at a new boyfriend's apartment so wasn't available as much as I should have been for the residents in my charge (who were all two years younger than I was but at the time might as well have been two decades. "Was I ever that young?" I would think as I looked at someone born eighteen months before me). This point is really driven home when one of my residents accidentally cuts off two of her fingers on an electric saw in scenic design class. Apparently they were trying to get in touch with me for several hours with no luck to meet her at the hospital. Again, no cell phones. It wasn't until the next day that I found out about it, and really it's not like I could've done much except help look for the fingers (which were later found and wonkily reattached). But I did feel badly. And I couldn't help but think it reflected poorly on my job performance when students started losing body parts. It also underlined how little I wanted to remain at NYU. I'd only gone to graduate school as a way to forestall joining the world, but I was ready now. Besides, I was only twenty-three, I didn't want to be responsible for a floor full of undergraduate students' shitty little lives. (Coincidentally, the law firm where my mother worked represented the fingerless student who ended up suing the university. A few days after I find this out I have a friend call the law firm and ask specifically to speak to my mother and tell her he was in this same class and cut off his ear and would they represent him as well. My mother later calls me and asks, "What's going on at that school?!")

I decide to leave NYU and focus on my acting career. Up until this time I hadn't quite decided if I was going to be a writer or an actor, since both seemed equally impossible it was almost like choosing between being an astrophysicist and a Navy SEAL.

I find out from another cater waiter that I work with (I'm a cater waiter part-time for most of my twenties. Being a cater waiter was very popular in the '90s if you were young and attractive and wanted to be an actor and were okay with being lightly molested by the older gay men that were inevitably your boss) about The William Esper Studio and decide to apply there. It is an acting school for people who are serious about their craft but not good enough to get into Juilliard or any place that you'd actually want to go to.

I audition and am accepted (anybody willing to write the check pretty much gets in, but I don't know that—but deep down I do) to the twice-weekly three-hour classes.

My teacher is a middle-aged man, Carl, who is appearing in an Off-Broadway revival of *I Can Get It for You Wholesale*, and I am immediately impressed.

Up until then I had only known one other person who had that much success. A young actress, Anne Bobby, who I did a summer workshop with at Oxford when I was nineteen who ended up starring on Broadway the following year in the musical *Smile*. (I go see the show and visit Anne backstage afterward. So other was this world I might as well have been dropped on Mars. And yet she fit so seamlessly into it, it seemed to me. With her robe and her throaty laugh and her hot water with lemon, all of eighteen years old. I wanted desperately to be a part of it as well, lounging in my dressing room, greeting visitors, receiving compliments, none of which are ever enough, more more more, swallowing them greedily like tiny hors d'oeuvres that can never satisfy. But instead I'm living in Queens with my parents and commuting to Hofstra while selling shoes part-time. The musical ends up being a huge flop and closes days after I see it, so that was some small consolation.)

The class is pretty evenly divided between men and women,

and I am to discover we are going to study a method of acting known as the Meisner technique. This was made popular in the '50s and was one of the earliest forms of method acting, which is basically acting like you're *not* acting, which usually has the end result of making you look like you're acting twice as hard. The classes consist of mostly improvisational work. We are to focus on our intent *not* on the words, therefore we won't be doing any typical scene work from, you know, actual plays. Perhaps I should've studied up on this school before committing a good chunk of my crappy cater waiter salary for the next year but it was a much bigger hassle back then to look into anything. I just assumed we'd be doing scenes from Neil Simon and David Mamet and I'd wear cute T-shirts and cut a sexy figure as I expertly spit out whatever lines I'd memorized the night before. I loved words and plays and reading and discussing and this was going to be none of that. We would be doing something called repetition exercises twice a week for the first year of the two-year program.

To start we were partnered with a classmate of the opposite sex and then taught the rules of the repetition exercise. Basically someone says a sentence like "Did you mail the letter?" and it gets repeated back and forth between the two of you until you want to kill yourself. (During rehearsal time you have to come up with what your relationship is with your partner and why each of you is so obsessed with this fucking letter. I am partnered with a pretty no-nonsense blonde, Amanda, who I like a lot. For some reason I don't remember telling her that

I'm gay. She obviously knew anyway so I guess it would've been redundant to tell her because we immediately determined our relationship was going to be brother and sister.)

This exercise quickly devolves into the men angrily screaming "Did you mail the letter?" and the women hysterically sobbing back "Did you mail the letter?" The class would inevitably find out later that the subtext had something to do with the end of their pretend relationship or someone cheating on someone. The louder the men screamed and the more the women cried the more our teacher, Carl, loved it. Hence more screaming and more crying.

I, on the other hand, could never get myself that upset over whatever imagined scenario we were acting out nor could I come up with a plausible reason why I would keep repeating the same fucking sentence like a lunatic instead of actually saying what was on my mind. But perhaps it was a shortcoming on my part that prevented me from screaming at Amanda at the top of my lungs, veins bulging from my neck, "DID YOU MAIL THE LETTER?!" while, sobbing and broken she sputtered back "Did you mail the letter?"

Week after week this went on. The sentences would change as would the pretend scenarios but the end result was basically the same. Men screaming, women crying, and me a kind of nonplussed observer. If this bothered Amanda she never mentioned it. Sometimes I would try to get myself really worked up but the best I was usually able to muster was extreme eye-rolling.

Carl would then critique each one of these exercises with the kind of self-seriousness only the truly deluded can pull off. As he talked about the inner life that each student was able to bring to the surface through repeating sentences like "I ran to the bus" a few dozen times I thought, "What the fuck am I missing?"

My critiques inevitably were tepid at best. "You're holding back" or "I didn't believe it" were the most popular. Yeah, I didn't fucking believe it either because it's ridiculous.

But I didn't want to give up. I had committed to a year. And our class had just found out that one of last year's graduates, Cady McClain, had booked a contract role on *All My Children* and was already nominated for a Soap Opera Digest Award as Best Newcomer. If this wasn't reason enough to remain in the program I don't know what was. The other students and I would talk about her in the kind of awed tones that Lee Strasberg's students must have talked about Marilyn Monroe. Any one of us could be next! (Cady McClain ends up spending over two decades on the show and creates one of the most iconic characters in soap history, Dixie Cooney, so good for you, Cady.)

I struggle through the entire first year. Along the way several students drop out but I remain—so committed am I to the possibility of a contract role on *All My Children*. (And the more discomfiting thought, if I leave this, then what?)

During the last week of the program Carl brings in a movement instructor who is going to manipulate our bodies as we perform our final repetition exercise. Only two couples are chosen for this demonstration, and much to my surprise Amanda and I are one of them. I am beyond nervous since the only emotion I've been able to show so far this year has been mild cuntyness. Amanda and I are called up and I seem to remember we are a brother and sister (surprise) dealing with our mother's death and trying to piece together a broken vase while repeating the sentence "I don't know what to do" and before I know it this movement instructor stands behind me and wraps his arms around me and within less than five seconds I'm sobbing uncontrollably "I don't know what to do." Amanda is startled and responds, frightened, "I don't know what to do." Now I'm wailing "I DON'T KNOW WHAT TO DO!" I notice other students looking uncomfortable. This goes on for a while. (I am so exhausted afterward I sleep that night for twelve hours.) Every cry that I've held in, every name that I've ever been called, every lunch that I've had to eat alone, every humiliation, every slight, everything is suddenly released in that one moment of connection. When I'm done, for the first time, Carl praises my performance. And I know I can never repeat it.

At the end of the year we are to have an evaluation from Carl and told whether or not we have been accepted into the second, more intense, year of the program. I'm not quite sure what could be more intense than just having had what amounts to a public nervous breakdown but, whatever, we're going to be working from actual scripts, and I figure the worst part is now behind me.

Carl tells me he is happy with the breakthrough I had during my last scene and before that he was going to recommend that I didn't continue in the program but now he was having second thoughts.

"I'm going to invite you back but you're going to have to do a lot of work."

Like what? I'm thinking, but I just smile and nod eagerly. He then tells me I look like a leading man but don't act like one. Of course all I hear is "I look like a leading man!" But I understand all too well the insidiousness of the comment. Basically the way I moved, the way I talked, everything about me, my whole essence was wrong. If I wanted to continue in the program I had to promise to take their movement and voice classes as well (for additional money that I didn't have but that's another thing). And as he's ticking off all my flaws I'm standing there thinking he wants to de-gay me. And to be an actor I think that's what I need to do. (This is before Matt Bomer and Jim Parsons and Neil Patrick Harris. There were gay characters in the '90s but they always had to be played by straight actors. To make them more palatable, I guess.) I realize this is essentially nothing more than conversion therapy for gay actors. And I say okay.

And I come back the following year and I find the money for the movement and the voice classes and I think, yes, let them turn me into a leading man. And my new second-year teacher is a woman, younger, and she talks about how we are going to address the way I walk, talk, etc., and in that moment I get up and say "I'm sorry, I'm leaving." I walk out and never return.

During the previous year I went with some other students from my class to see Carl in the Off-Broadway revival of *I Can Get It for You Wholesale*. (The show that made Barbra Streisand a star. You should know this. She sings one number, "Miss Marmelstein," and stops the show. She's nineteen. Go listen to it.) Carl has a small part (there *are* small parts, by the way), and something tells me that he's only fine, nothing special, he's not anything other than a struggling mediocre actor who never made it, but at the time I push that feeling away and now, as I exit The William Esper Studio for the last time it comes back. Strong and sharp and mean. "He stinks. Fuck him."

I walk back, alone, to my apartment. I don't know what to do. I don't know what to do.

QE2

I am seventeen years old. There is a senior trip to Hawaii during Easter break and my parents tell me they will pay for the trip as a graduation present. I pass on the offer. After four years I still haven't found someone to walk to the cafeteria with much less travel five thousand miles with.

It's not that I don't love to travel. My family has been going on cruises since I was born. My father works for Cunard Line and gets two free trips a year. My mom would pull us out of school for some of them, and we would bring back a little ceramic figurine or bottle of rum for our teachers. This was the '70s so you could pretty much come and go as you pleased. At the time most of the ships left from Manhattan so we'd just take our car into the city and leave it in a garage at the pier. Driving underneath the huge bow of the *QE2* as it hung over the West Side Highway waiting to take us out of the cold and into the tropics. Once in our cabin, my sister and I would immediately check the daily program to find out who the entertainers were. We went often enough that we had our favorites. But no one made us freak the fuck out more than Jay Romaine. Jay Romaine was a puppeteer who operated large wooden marionettes and made them dance while wearing a black turtleneck. One was a Mae West–type puppet named Boob Boobs LaRue, who he made strut suggestively (each boob moving independently) to "Great Balls of Fire." When Jay Romaine performed, the Double Down Room on board the *QE2* was packed, every seat taken. Cigarette smoke filled the air, ice cubes clinked. My sister and I would sit on the steps of the huge curved staircase that cut through the center of the lounge and watch mesmerized through the clear glass railing. Opening night of *Hamilton* could not have been more thrilling. There was also a comedian we loved. Marty Frawley. He was Irish and sat on a stool in a tuxedo and told jokes while downing cocktails, slurring hilariously by the end of the show. Alcoholism was, for some reason, utterly charming in the '70s. Days on island beaches, evenings roaming the ship, bingo, movies, midnight buffets, it was a stark contrast to my normal daily life of hiding in stairwells and eating lunch alone in the library. I came to live for those two weeks a year and the rest of the time I lay dormant, biding my time, waiting, until the inevitable day one of my parents would casually mention over dinner that we were going on a cruise. And just like that I could feel myself coming alive again.

It is now several weeks before our Easter break and my father says, since I'm not going on the senior trip to Hawaii would I like to go on a cruise. He tells me I'd have to go by myself as both he and my mother are unable to get off work (my sister, in college now, has other interests, the cruises no longer taking up the central part of her brain, unlike mine). I quickly say yes.

On the day of the trip my father drives me to the pier and accompanies me on board the *QE2*. I find it very impressive that he can flash the kind of credentials that allowed a person to stroll right onto a cruise ship whenever they wanted. He walks me to my cabin and helps me hang my clothes in the small closet. The dinner jacket I will need for the captain's cocktail party, my slacks for casual nights, sweaters for cool evenings at sea. And before long the bells chime, indicating those not sailing needed to head ashore.

I go up on deck with all the other passengers to watch us set sail. As we pull out of the harbor I spot my father in the parking lot getting into his Caprice Classic. I wave but he doesn't see me, and at no point does it seem odd to me that a seventeen-year-old boy is leaving on a ten-day cruise to the Caribbean by himself.

I'm assigned to dine at a table with a middle-aged couple celebrating their anniversary, the woman who will be giving lectures on scarf-tying, and a legal secretary who has been carrying on an affair with one of the ship's officers. I sit next to the scarf-tying woman and we hit it off immediately. (I couldn't string two words together if you sat me next to a classmate in the cafeteria, but put me on a cruise ship and sit me next to a divorced forty-year-old woman and I couldn't shut up.) The legal secretary smokes and drinks gin and tonics and talks of a life spent going to restaurants and Manhattan nightclubs. When the French purser she's been secretly seeing stops by our table to whisper in her ear I decide she is easily the most glamorous person I have ever met.

A few days later I will see the legal secretary in one of the shops on board. I will approach her, and when she turns to me she is crying. She tells me she had a fight with the ship's purser and that she's afraid he's losing interest in her. She met him five years ago on her first cruise and since then has spent all of her savings visiting him several times a year. She quickly apologizes and tells me she's just being stupid and of course he still cares for her. And we make a plan, for later that afternoon, to enter the Trivial Pursuit competition together.

On the last night of the trip, when I see the legal secretary outside the card room, she is in the arms of the ship's purser and she is kissing him and I see the small purse she is carrying slip from her fingers onto the floor. I bend to pick it up. She catches my eye, and somehow I know to leave it there. I never see her again because she doesn't come to breakfast the following morning.

But on the first night she is laughing. And we are celebrating the middle-aged couple's anniversary. They order a bottle of champagne from the wine steward and we toast them. The scarf-tying woman is wearing my blazer because it is chilly in the restaurant. She wears it draped over her bare shoulders and has, not unexpectedly, knotted the sleeves very smartly across her chest.

(A few tables away I spot a couple in their fifties sitting alone with a teddy bear that wears a bow tie and dinner jacket. The teddy bear sits atop several books stacked onto his chair and faces a formal place setting. Throughout the meal I see the couple occasionally address the bear, forcing the waiter to acknowledge him as well. I mention this to my tablemates, and we all take notice, excitedly watching each subsequent evening as the bear shows up to dinner in a different outfit. On the night of the captain's cocktail party I see the couple with him in the Double Down Room. They wait in line along with the other passengers to greet the captain. When it is their turn, the bear, now in a tuxedo, is introduced to the captain by the woman. Prompted by her he politely shakes its tiny paw. And as they all pose for the ship's photographer it is suddenly no longer amusing, like so many things that start out funny and end up just sad.)

When I walk into the dining room several days later I am the last to arrive. The others have waited for me and we take turns talking about our day onshore. The middle-aged couple went exploring, and the wife pulls her hair back to show me the earrings she bought in town. The scarf-tying woman had to stay on board to give her lecture. We do not ask if the legal secretary has gone ashore because by now we know that she never leaves the ship. She waits in her cabin until the purser calls to tell her that he is free. On a previous cruise she once went ashore to buy a straw bag in St. Lucia and he became angry. She tells me this on the day we meet in the shop.

When it is my turn I tell them I went to a local beach and read. I do not tell them that while I'm on the beach I see one of the dancers from the ship. Blond and lean he recognizes me and asks if he can join me and I say yes.

His legs are muscular from months of dancing at sea and he has the bland good looks of someone who is handsome at twenty but will not be at thirty. Lying on the sand this close to him I am excited in a way I imagine only the legal secretary would understand. Here I am on the beach in Barbados spending the day with a dancer from the *QE2*. I could never have dreamed such a thing for myself. I will travel with him around the world. Visiting outdoor markets and ancient ruins during the days and helping him with his dance routines in the late afternoons. Each night I will sit in the audience and watch as he spins his Russian dance partner through the air and think "he belongs to me."

But nothing happens on the beach and we barely speak. The dancer buys us each a Coke and I sip it slowly, too nervous to say even thank you.

I am about to ask the middle-aged couple what they are planning to do in Antigua tomorrow when all of the waiters come out of the kitchen carrying Baked Alaskas lit with sparklers. Our conversation ends as we all get caught up in the excitement.

After I leave the dining room I go to the Double Down Room to watch that night's show. And he is there, twirling his dance partner across the floor to Donna Summer, and I look at him in a way that I couldn't when he was lying right next to me.

When it's over I walk back to my cabin and read the daily program, deciding what I will do the next day.

(I go on several cruises over the next few years, and then, just like that, I stop. Like someone who has too long worked in an ice cream shop and can no longer stomach the sight of it. But then, years later, the craving returns. A little voice: "It's time." And I am in my forties now and my boyfriend and I fly to Istanbul to join the *Silver Spirit* on a cruise through the Mediterranean. And when I see the ship I am giddy again. Once in our cabin, as I did for so many years with my sister Maria, I pick up the daily program and there it is—performing on this voyage will be Jay Romaine. And I think, it can't be. Jay Romaine with the marionettes from thirty years ago? I call my sister immediately, so excited we squeal on the phone, suddenly children. And then it's time to set sail. I tell my boyfriend, Brad, about the puppets and sitting in the Double Down Room on the *QE2* with Maria and how magical these evenings were and that I can't wait to be able to share it with him. He tells me you have to tell him that you grew up watching him perform and what it meant to you. Yes, yes, I respond, of course, it's all too perfect. The universe has brought me to this moment. I decide I will chat with him after his show, so much to say. It's not until days later when I see the daily program announcing "An Evening with Jay Romaine" that I believe this is actually happening.

Brad and I get to the ship's lounge early. I wait for it to fill up. And as it gets closer to showtime I realize it's not going to. There are maybe a dozen or so of us scattered throughout the room. Before he even comes on my heart begins to sink. The curtain opens and he's standing there, still in his black turtleneck but now an old man, holding Boob Boobs LaRue. And this puppet looks cheap, and worn, and dirty and just then a tinny version of "Great Balls of Fire" comes over the speakers and already people are starting to leave.

The next number is one that I didn't even know I remembered, but the second it starts it comes flooding back to me. It's about a little mouse that lived in a house behind the stairs and he gets married to another little mouse and they have children and the puppets keep multiplying and multiplying, one mouse after another, until Jay Romaine, in a triumphant performance, is manipulating seven marionettes, each seemingly produced out of thin air. On board the *QE2* this number got an ovation, hundreds of people loudly applauding him. Now, on board the *Silver Spirit*, I turn to Brad and whisper "let's go" before he even gets to the third mouse.

I see him several times after this throughout the ship. But I don't say anything to him. I don't even look at him. I can't.)

I'D LIKE TO THANK

Wow! This is so unexpected! Oh, God, I don't even have anything prepared! Please don't play me off, orchestra! I guess the first thing I want to say is to everybody at St. Mel's grammar school in Flushing, Queens, fuck you. This award is made so much sweeter by the fact that I know none of you have accomplished anything with your lives. I guess some of you have. Like maybe a few of you became doctors or lawyers but nothing that you're winning an Oscar for. I particularly want to single out one specific asshole—I hope you're watching Joseph Spicallini because ever since that day that you erased the R in my name off the blackboard leaving just the G A Y I've been planning this. Did it feel good to have the whole class laugh at your little joke? I bet it did. It was so fucking hilarious. What a wit you were. You humiliated me in front of twenty-five people that day. Forgive me for taking forty years to respond, Joseph, but I wanted to wait until I had a global audience of roughly 750 million people. When I walked home from school that day so many years ago I didn't cry. I started plotting. The next years were spent observing, studying, watching. Every little bit of every nothing I studied and turned over like a stone until it became smooth and slick. When you're trying to remain invisible so as to avoid further humiliations, further shame, you notice a lot of things. Small details that might not capture the attention of anyone else. And then when I was eighteen I was finally born. And I was better-looking than you were, and smarter, and cleverer, with a survival instinct that had been honed by years of expecting nothing and knowing I had to work for everything I got. And then I came out and I found love and I lost love and I found it again and I waited and I waited and I waited and I started writing and I never forgot. And all those things I observed and watched and saw, gave me a point of view, a personality, an attitude. It gave me something to draw from, Joseph. And I wrote more and I wrote more. When you keep everything inside you for eighteen years you find you have a lot to say when the time finally presents itself. And I waited and I waited. You become good at waiting when you're gay. Waiting to come out, waiting to meet someone, waiting for the other shoe to drop, waiting for your rights, waiting. And I wrote more and I read and I traveled and I got older. Waiting, waiting, waiting. I worked hard and wouldn't stop writing. I took every job, every opportunity, because this was what I was driving toward, Joseph, this moment. I saw on Facebook that you're divorced and have three kids, two of which have been in and out of rehab and one that lives in your basement. I'm not on Facebook but I'd check in on you occasionally. From the best I can make out from your profile you sell above-ground swimming pools on Long Island for a living. Now for anybody out there watching this who is NOT Joseph Spicallini and also sells above-ground swimming pools on Long Island I'd like to apologize if you think I am, in any way, looking down on people who sell above-ground swimming pools. That is not my intention. My intention, rather, is merely to point out that I have a fucking Oscar and Joseph Spicallini sells above-ground swimming pools on Long Island. I can't imagine you expected your life to turn out this way, Joseph. But perhaps I should've done more to help you at the time—when we were both so young and so much still lay ahead of us. Perhaps I should have viciously tormented you over the course of eight years. Made you feel off-balance for most of your childhood. That would've given you a thick skin, you see. Something to push back against. Let you know you weren't special, you weren't entitled to anything, and you were going to have to develop skills you didn't know you had in order to survive, persevere, and then, ultimately, thrive. But I didn't do that. How could I, really? And you went on, growing bolder, more smug, crueler, never looking at the world from outside but always from your privileged vantage point. Nothing to prove, nothing to achieve, nothing to desire. No ambition, drive, no aspirations, dreams, objectives.

Complacent. Mediocre. Average. Now I'm not going to mention that you've lost most of your hair. Or that you're fat. Because this is 2019 and I don't want to body shame anyone. Isn't it ironic? I'm refusing to mention how fat and almost unrecognizable you've become, your features seemingly puffed out from the bloat of alcohol until you more closely resemble a parade balloon than your thirteen-year-old self when you called me faggot almost every day for eight years with no thought whatsoever for my feelings. But I'm more sensitive than you, I guess. I refuse to stoop to your level, Joseph Spicallini. What's strange, though, is that we were friends in first grade. And I think second grade, too. I don't know when it turned exactly. But it was always going to. I suppose I always knew it was just a matter of time before people would see what was really inside of me and that it wouldn't go well after that. I used to fantasize sometimes that you would call to apologize, and in that call it would somehow undo all the damage that had been done. But I'm grateful for it. That's why I'd like to thank you, Joseph Spicallini. Because without you I wouldn't be up here tonight. Has this all seemed so very petty? Do I sound like a small person? Someone who cannot forgive? I don't really care. I've given up caring what anyone thinks of me a long time ago. Because you don't win fucking Academy Awards caring what other people think about you. Well, maybe Julie Andrews did. She seems like she cares what other people think about her. But nobody else. Sally Field. Her, too. But that's it. You know what they say, revenge is a dish best served from the Oscar podium.

Wow. It just hit me. I don't know what I'm going to do after this. I don't really know what's going to motivate me now. But I'm sure there are other people I need to get back at, people who've really fucked me over, and it's time I start focusing my energy on them. I'm coming for all of you, fuckers. Good night! Oh, and I'd also like to thank my agent Jay Sures at UTA!

BETTER BODIES

In the '90s the only way to meet guys was at the gym. Whether or not you wanted to work out wasn't an option. It was pretty much mandatory. Now you get to have all different kinds of gays—hipster, skinny, fat—and nobody cares. That wasn't allowed then. If you didn't have a body you might as well not have been gay. And your body needed to be perfect. I worked out two hours a day six days a week starting when I was twenty-two. It's not like I wanted to or even enjoyed it, I didn't have a choice. I wish I could be twenty-two now and be the kind of gay that was scrawny and bookish and sexy, but that didn't cut it then. The first thing anybody ever said to you was, "What gym do you go to?" Also popular: "I know him from the gym" "I used to go to that gym" "How is that gym?" "I've seen you at the gym" and "He doesn't go to my gym."

And it was only gay people who went to the gym. Straight guys didn't work out then. Unless you were a model or in the Olympics. And for some reason, I don't know why, in the early '90s all gay men shaved their legs. I didn't. Mostly because I couldn't be bothered. But I would be the only one. And everyone wore white Hanes tank tops and baseball caps. And everyone mostly worked out only their upper bodies. And wore weight belts and weight-lifting gloves. And listened to Discmans. If you wanted to talk to someone you waited until they were changing CDs. And you worked out at night. And you didn't worry about form or your core because those things didn't exist yet. You bench-pressed as much weight as you could and you bounced the barbell on your chest to get the momentum to lift it. And you swung the dumbbells when doing bicep curls. You did whatever you had to do to lift that fucking weight. And you would always think everyone else's body was better than your own. The highest compliment I've ever received to this day was "How do you get your arms like that?" "*My* arms? You want to know how I get *my* arms like this?" I was used to trying to get my body to look like everyone else's, it had never occurred to me that there might be someone who was trying to get their body to look like *mine*.

And you paid your gym membership before you paid your rent. It was the number one most important thing to have. My gym was Better Bodies and it was in a basement in Chelsea and *everyone* went there. We called it Bitter Beauties. We changed the names to all the gyms then. The David Barton Gym was The

Dolly Parton Gym and the Bally's Health Club over the D'Agostino supermarket on the Upper West Side was Fags over D'Ags. Now people go to Equinox and call it Equinox.

We were forced to go to the gym mostly because of Calvin Klein underwear ads in the '80s. We all collectively decided that this was the body of choice and stopped at nothing until we had it. And it took a lot of time. There were no supplements around (except steroids which were frowned upon then as cheating), so you had to do everything yourself.

And when you met someone at the gym, as you inevitably would, someone would have to give someone their phone number. I always preferred to *get* the phone number so that I could call the person myself (it also allowed me to act a bit coy, as if I wasn't sure I wanted to give out my number, something so personal, but I'll take *your* number—now you see each other's dicks before you even have coffee but then it was like the Dance of the Seven Veils), but the truth was I didn't want to be the one waiting by the phone, which was its own special hell that thank God no longer exists.

And here's a fantastic thing that would happen. This person that you had maybe seen at the gym for months or weeks or just today and now he's writing his phone number down on a ripped-off piece of paper (the front desks always had pens and paper for just such moments), and you fold it up and put it in your gym shorts (cutoff sweats) and later you take it out and unfold it and it is like he is there again. The slip of paper with the number on it has now been replaced by Grindr and

Scruff and Instagram but nothing, nothing can be as exciting as walking back to your apartment and climbing the stairs and unlocking the door and reaching into your pocket and pulling out that tiny slip of paper and looking at his handwriting. How he writes his sevens his fours his eights. And a little bit of him is there with you. And it's thrilling. Because this paper is a contract that tells you something happened. A moment. A brief moment recognizing that you had been seen. And this paper could hold your future. This could be the piece of paper you keep for fifty years. The paper that you will show him when you're old and the excitement of that moment is long gone but something better is left in its place. A lifetime. And you will show him this tiny slip of paper when you're both old and gray and say "do you know what this is" and he will say "oh, my God, you saved it" and you will say "of course I saved it" and when you unfold that paper it will take you back to that day when you were both young men and it will be like you entered a time machine, this tiny piece of paper—your very own Proust's madeleine, your most valued possession. It will remind you of everything. Your entire life is in this paper. The way he makes his sevens his fours his eights.

But this doesn't happen of course. This tiny piece of paper gets put in your wallet. And you call him and leave a message and don't hear from him or you do and go out and it's weird or it's not and any number of things happen that isn't a lifetime together and you keep the tiny piece of paper in your wallet longer than you should because once you throw it away you're also throwing away the possibility. But you eventually *do* throw it away. Usually on the same day you get a new tiny piece of paper with a new phone number. And again you look at it and think "he wrote this" and it seems like the most intimate thing in the world, this piece of paper, and you put it somewhere safe. And you hope.

BENNIGAN'S

When I'm in college on Long Island I get a job as a waiter at Bennigan's. The tagline for the restaurant is "when you're hungry for fun." Having seen the kitchen, it was definitely more appropriate than "when you're hungry for food." It was the '80s, and preppy was very big. We all dressed like extras in a John Hughes movie. I was twenty and had never waited tables before. To me just going out to dinner seemed like the height of sophistication. To think that *I* was going to be a waiter. Your guide through an evening of glamour and decadence. I imagined something out of Dorothy Parker or the Weimar Republic. Groups of artists and intellectuals and famous wits holding court and me swanning in and out with trays of canapés and buckets of champagne. Sinuously weaving my way through the tables as if I were performing a dance routine that had been choreographed by Bob Fosse. A graceful creature who would become a source of endless fascination and desire. I am your host! *Willkommen, bienvenue, welcome, im Bennigan's, au Bennigan's, to Bennigan's!*

Instead, I find myself within several days of getting the job crouched over a trash can in the kitchen stuffing a handful of someone's uneaten french fries into my mouth. (This was, unfortunately, going to be a somewhat lower-budget experience than I had originally anticipated.)

On my first day the manager instructs me that I am under no circumstances to eat any of the food off of a customer's plate. This is something I am to find out is called "garbage mouthing." I am appalled that this manager would think that under any circumstance I would consider stooping to something so revolting. "Uh, you don't have to worry about me," I say, so fucking offended. What kind of animal eats off a stranger's plate in a restaurant? It's amazing how quickly you can be reduced to your most base instincts. Something that heretofore seemed unimaginable can become commonplace in basically the blink of an eye. Doing it the first time was the worst. Probably not unlike murder. But after that it becomes a lot easier.

Let me walk you through how someone who doesn't even like to sip from a friend's straw finds himself eating a hamburger that already has several bites taken out of it.

During the '80s there wasn't anything to my knowledge known as "workers' rights," and shifts were extraordinarily long. Children sewing buttons in Chinese sweatshops got more break time than the waiters at the Great Neck Bennigan's. We were to eat before our shift began. I usually worked from 4:00 P.M. to 2:00 A.M., and it would pass in a fever dream. Each shift seemed to last a lifetime, encompassing all the emotions that go with it. Joy, sorrow, fear, despair. Perhaps the time would have gone by faster if I had ever gotten any good at the job.

If you're a waiter who has fallen behind and is frantically trying to play catch-up it is called being "in the weeds." I was never *not* in the weeds. If someone ordered tea for three people it was a time-consuming chore that I could never come back from. I'd still be making up for it the next day. Now something as benign as a cup of tea you would think would be the easiest thing in the world to put together, and in theory it should be. Except each order of tea came with its own little pot of boiling water, and loose-leaf tea, and a tea strainer with its own holder, and little containers of honey and sugar and milk. You'd think we were at fucking Buckingham Palace. It was like trying to put together a thousand-piece jigsaw puzzle of blue sky. The twenty minutes it would take me to prepare a tea order meant I would fall so far behind in everything else that I could never recover. I was perpetually on the verge of hysteria. The only thing worse than someone ordering a cup of tea was someone ordering a bottle of wine. (Now I had gone out to eat growing up, usually Chinese food, pizza, the occasional steak house, and if my parents had ever ordered a bottle of wine, I would've dropped dead of shock. I don't think

I'd ever seen anyone do it except on *Dynasty*.) First, I would get incredibly nervous—"A bottle of wine?! These people are rich!"—and then I was afraid they would God forbid ask me for a recommendation. I didn't drink wine, nor did I know anything about it, including how to open it. Once, while struggling with a bottle tableside, I actually cried. I can still feel their eyes on me as I wrestled with it, you'd think I was trying to get a cat into a bathtub, my frozen smile quickly giving way to total anguish. I didn't show as much emotion when my grandmother died. Being perpetually panicked allowed no time to take even a five-minute break. And after about six, seven hours of going nonstop the hunger would become too much and suddenly I'd find myself eyeing up the customers to determine whose plate I'd eat off of. "She seems clean. He's only eating from one side of the dish. Nobody's gone anywhere near those chicken fingers." And then, after having cleared the table, I'd go through the swinging doors into the kitchen, hunch over the trash can, and begin shoveling the uneaten food into my mouth as fast as I could. When the door would once again swing open I'd look up, frozen in fear, with half a baked potato sticking out of my mouth, and when I'd see it was just another waiter I'd resume my pose over the trash can and continue frantically shoveling it down my throat. Raccoons had more dignity than I did.

And I had no waiter friends to help me out. I didn't have the luxury of time to make waiter friends. I didn't even have any space in my brain to learn their names, so intent was I on focusing all my energy on just getting through the shift. Normally waiters would help each other out but *only* if you were in a position to also help them out when they needed it. I had never been operating in any mode other than hysterical so was in no position to even make eye contact with another waiter much less help them bring food out when they were in the weeds. And nothing underscored this point more than when you had a table with a birthday. If I had seen battle in Vietnam I would still wake up screaming from dreams of having to get other waiters to help me with a table celebrating a birthday.

A birthday at Bennigan's was a big event, they were kind of known for it. Usually it'd go like this: someone at the table would whisper to you "it's Bill's birthday" and then you would go to the kitchen, get the special birthday cake (I can still taste it, so many handfuls of chocolate eaten over so many trash cans), light the candles, and ask whatever waiters you could round up to come out and sing with you the Bennigan's birthday song. *Happy happy birthday on this your special day/ Happy happy birthday that's what we're here to say/Happy happy birthday—may all your dreams come true/Happy happy birthday from Bennigan's to you! Hey!*

Now I had never come out and sung with any other waiters when they had a birthday, so it only goes to follow that no other waiters ever wanted to come out with me when I had a birthday. I wanted to help out the other waiters when they had a birthday, I did, because it looked fun to join in (the more popular the waiter, the more people who came out to sing with them, arms around each other, joking, smiling), and I also knew that then they would be in my debt when I had a birthday, but I could never get my shit together enough to give up the two minutes it would cost me, so I just looked down when someone would come into the kitchen yelling "I've got a birthday!" Others will help them, I thought, they'll be fine.

And then, a few minutes later, someone sitting at my station would inevitably whisper while pointing conspiratorially to the person across from them "it's Pam's birthday," and I would die inside. I would then have to return to the kitchen. "I have a birthday." Nothing. Nobody would even look at me. I would become increasingly more agitated: "Guys, I have a birthday, come on!" Still nothing. "I can't go back out there alone! Someone help me, I'm begging you!" No one would even lift their head. It was like I wasn't even there. They all hated me. But there was one waiter, I still remember him, tall and handsome in a frat boy way, who would waltz through his shift as though it were as easy as breathing, and he would wordlessly walk through the swinging doors with me and the two of us would stand there *Happy happy birthday on this your special day/Happy happy birthday that's what we're here to say/ Happy happy birthday—may all your dreams come true/Happy happy birthday from Bennigan's to you! Hey!*

When it was over he would immediately walk away. As quickly as he came into my life that's how quickly he would depart it. Sometimes we would be joined by a third waiter, and once, even a fourth. And at that moment, that only time, I felt a part of something. Standing there with my brothers and sisters, supported, loved, understood, each of us there for the other. I would get the hang of this. (I don't.) I would learn names. I would not only become capable, I would excel. (I don't.) I would come to the aid of my fellow waiters. I would master all tasks. (I quit a few weeks later.) I would stop garbage mouthing. I would restore my dignity. I would look back on this time and laugh. (Never happens.) I would learn about wine. I would arrive early and stay late. I would be everyone's favorite. I would tell stories of how difficult it was for me when *I* first started. People would be incredulous. "You?" "Me," I'd modestly respond. "But you're the best one here! We all look up to you!" And then someone new, someone just starting, would frantically burst through the swinging doors, just as I had so many times before, yelling "I have a birthday!" And I would calmly put my hand on his shoulder, grab a cake, and lead the parade of waiters out into the dining room, all of us singing as one.

ONE LIFE TO LIVE

I'm twelve years old when I decide to become addicted to a soap opera. I'm home sick from school, and feel like it's time I graduated from game shows to something with a little more substance. This is the '70s so there are many soaps to choose from. I thumb through *TV Guide*. (My bible—the day the Fall Preview issue arrives at our Queens mailbox I safeguard it in my room like a Fabergé egg. Saving each special issue to contrast and compare as the decade goes on. If a new show had a full-page ad in the Fall Preview issue, the network had high hopes for it let me fucking tell you, I knew that at six.) *Search for Tomorrow, The Doctors, Another World, The Edge of Night,* each conjuring up its own little universe filled with attractive, affluent, troubled people. I choose *One Life to Live*. I don't know why. It airs at 2:00 P.M. on channel 7. I will watch it for thirty-three years.

The first episodes I watch I can recall as if I'd just seen them yesterday. Karen Wolek (wife of Larry Wolek, Llanview's leading doctor and pillar of the community) is taking the stand in Victoria Lord's murder trial. Karen is played by Judith Light and she was giving a tour de force performance. In these scenes the town (along with me) are to discover that the perfect doctor's wife was, in reality, a prostitute. Karen delivers a monologue that lasts about a week. This was the craziest fucking thing I'd ever heard in my life and I was hooked.

I feel like you should go to YouTube and search "Karen Wolek takes the stand" before reading further so you'll have a better appreciation of what I'm talking about. It went on to become one of the most legendary scenes in soap opera history. And for good reason. Judith Light is SERVING IT. Mascara smeared, snot running down her face, hair insane (this was before the art of blow-drying had been perfected, so there was less pressure then on what was deemed TV acceptable. In today's parlance, she looked like a hot mess).

I didn't miss one episode the first year. My favorite characters were Victoria Lord (played by Erika Slezak, the Meryl Streep of daytime) the sainted, wealthy daughter of newspaper magnate Victor Lord, and her stepmother and eternal nemesis, Dr. Dorian Lord (played by Robin Strasser, heaven. Robin Strasser had previously starred on *Another World* where she played that show's popular heroine, Rachel. When I was very young, before my mother went to work in Manhattan, she would watch *Another World* each day, usually while ironing or folding laundry, and I would catch glimpses, stealing little bits occasionally, and then something happened on the show that she didn't like and she stopped watching it. Forever. Just like that. After watching it every day. She did the same thing years later with *Knots Landing*. "This is stupid," she'd announce and that would be it. She'd never watch again. I could not have imagined such a thing. Sometimes I still look at her and think, "What did *Another World* ever do to you?")

Viki and Dorian would go at it for decades. (Viki suffered from multiple personalities, and Dorian was a bitch. I, unsurprisingly, was drawn more to Dorian. Much as I had always watched *The Wizard of Oz* for the Wicked Witch of the West and *One Hundred and One Dalmatians* for Cruella De Vil. The cuntier the better as far as I was concerned.)

I would return home from school every day by two and immediately take the TV from my bedroom and place it on the kitchen table. I would turn on the show as I prepared my lunch (a fried egg on a roll or a pizza bagel made in the toaster oven) and then sit watching, transfixed. I didn't have anyone to eat with at school so I would wait until I got home to have lunch.

During that first year, while watching at the kitchen table, there was a storyline on *One Life to Live* where Pat Ashley, the host of Llanview's very own "The Pat Ashley Show" (produced by Dorian Lord, she was busy), gets visited by her British sister, Maggie, who ends up falling in love with Pat's boyfriend, Clint, and then kidnaps Pat and takes over her identity. It is about this time in the story, *months* into it, that I realize the actress who plays Pat, Jacqueline Courtney, is playing both parts. How was this even possible?? In the forty years since I cannot remember being as utterly surprised by *anything* as the day I realized Pat and Maggie were both being played by *the same person*. It was the most remarkable magic trick I could have imagined. ("Hey, waaaaait a minute . . . ," I said to myself when Maggie put on a blond wig to impersonate Pat and stopped talking in her British accent. The expression "the penny dropped" has never been more apt.) And this actress, who is long dead, will never know that because of it she has always held a special place in my heart. Will anything ever again make me feel as satisfied and as thrilled as I did in that moment when I first realized Pat and Maggie were being played by the same person? No, I don't think so.

It was a glorious two years of moving the TV into the kitchen for lunch. Why would I want to eat with anyone but the women of Llanview? School was just marking time until I could come home, take my TV out of my room, plop it onto the kitchen table, and sit eating my egg in peace with my favorite people. My parents both worked, and my sister had friends, hung out at school, had a life. At twelve I was basically a middle-aged woman. Counting calories, drinking Tab, watching my stories. This hour was *my* time.

During one of these lunches our doorbell rang. I hated to be disturbed during *One Life to Live* and was quite put out as

I answered the door. I didn't recognize the woman standing there. She was very distraught. Crying, upset. She tells me she is my neighbor Didi's sister. I did not even know Didi had a sister. And now she wants me to follow her to my neighbor's house. It seems Didi has fallen. Didi has Lou Gehrig's disease and I haven't seen her in a long time. When I was little she was always so nice to me and I remember after she first got sick she would be on her front porch, with her husband, in a wheelchair and we would go over and say "hi" and she could still talk and smile and then suddenly we didn't see her any-more and nobody really talked about it and now her sister is on our porch crying and I run out and I follow her. Didi had always been very clean and tidy and carried herself with such dignity. I remember having to take off my shoes when I had to go into her house for whatever reason. I hadn't been in it that many times but it was identical to ours. Always strange seeing how the exact same house could look so different when other lives were being lived inside. And I follow her sister into what would've been *my* sister's room and Didi is lying on the floor and she looks terrified and I can tell she is embarrassed for me to see her like this and I want to communicate to her that she shouldn't be. And I try to help her back into her bed and she moans like I am hurting her (and is she also crying now?) and I don't know what I should do but somehow I get her back into the bed and her sister has calmed down and Didi can no longer speak or move but her eyes are alert and alive and she looks at me, *really* looks at me, and I say something lame like "it's okay, Didi" and then she looks away moaning softly now, as if she cannot look at me anymore this has been too intimate for what our relationship has always been I am too young and the sister walks me to the door and thanks me and I leave and return to my identical house and the kitchen table where *One Life to Live* is still on and my egg sandwich sits unfinished and I watch the rest of the show. (I never see Didi again. Or her sister. Or talk about this.)

And then, when I'm fourteen, something extraordinary happens. My father, who works in sales for Cunard Line, returns from a business trip and tells me that one of the travel agents he works with has a brother who is on *One Life to Live*.

"What?? Who does he play, who's her brother?" I'm frantic.

"His name is Phil Carey, do you know him?" he asks.

Phil Carey?! Do I know him?! Phil Carey played Asa Buchanan, the most powerful person in all of Llanview, a Texas oilman, he was a millionaire (in the '70s a millionaire was impressive, now it's like being a teacher) and the head of Buchanan Industries of course I fucking knew Phil Carey!

"Yeah, he's Asa," I say. "What did she tell you about him?"

"I don't know, he doesn't like doing the show," he says.

He doesn't like doing the show?! How could he not like doing the show?! He's fucking Asa Buchanan! "Oh," I say, deflated.

A few weeks later he returns from another business trip where he sees Asa's sister again and I pump him for more information.

"He doesn't know how long he wants to stay on the show," he tells me.

He can't leave! He's Asa! (He ends up doing it for twenty-eight years, so . . .)

"The next time you see her do you think you can ask her to ask him if I can visit the set?" And he surprises me by saying okay. So I wait another month and he returns again after seeing her and says, "She said alright."

"I can go? Just like that?"

"I guess."

"Don't I need a pass or an invitation or something written?"

"Just tell him his sister knows your dad."

"When do I go?"

"I don't know."

And I know not to push him any further. Besides, I have more than enough to work with, I figure.

First I need to find out where they film *One Life to Live*. Today it would take you all of three seconds, but then you had to dig around. I buy something called *The Ross Reports*, a booklet that comes out every so often that tells you where they shoot all the TV shows. Just holding it was like being in possession of a key that promised entry into a secret room. *One Life to Live* was filmed at 56 West Sixty-sixth Street in Manhattan, I discover. Strange that an entire town could be contained in such a small address. I go with a friend of mine from school, Toni. She is sweet and also a fan of the show (but not like me, no one was like me) and is impressed when I ask her if she'd like to go with me on a tour of the studio.

We take the subway into the city on a day off from school. I don't really have a plan and Toni is unaware how flimsy my connection to the show really is. We arrive at the studio, which basically looks like any brownstone on the Upper West Side. I walk into the lobby and introduce myself to the guard like I own the place. "Hi, I'm here to see Phil Carey."

"Is he expecting you?"

"No, but his sister said I can come whenever." Hearing it come out of my mouth I'm starting to get a little nervous. He's at lunch I'm told. Everyone is. I'll have to wait until he comes back. "What did he say?" Toni asks.

"We just have to wait until he gets back from lunch," I say confidently. And so we stand outside the studio, waiting. And they start coming back, the actors. Singly. In pairs. Karen! And Jenny and Marco! Edwina! It's all too much! I smile eagerly, hoping one of them will say "Aren't you the son of the man who knows Phil's sister the travel agent?" But, of course, none do. And then, suddenly, I see him, Phil Carey, walking down Sixty-sixth Street. I get a sick feeling in my stomach but I walk right up to him.

"Hi, my name is Gary. My dad knows your sister and she said you'd give us a tour." I'm not saying he looks like he's going to hit me because I'm only a child but he doesn't *not* look like he's going to hit me. I'd be hard-pressed to remember a time when I'd been looked at with that much disgust. I believe his exact words were "leave me alone, kid" or something to that effect and he keeps walking and enters the studio.

Toni says, "I guess we should go." Do you think I'm fucking leaving without getting in there? They'll have to drag me by my feet, my bloodied nails dug into the sidewalk. And then I see the actress who plays Samantha Vernon approaching (this was the second actress to play Samantha and she is new to the show, I loved the first one and was a bit lukewarm on the recast to be honest so I wasn't as excited as I would've been if, say, it were the *real* Samantha, but anyway) and I go up to her and I tell her my story.

Then she says "hold on" and goes into the building and talks to the security guard while we wait outside. A few minutes later she returns, "come on, kids," and we enter the building with her. She addresses the guard, "These are my guests." And I remember being not as surprised as I actually should have been. Like I expected it to work out exactly as it had. Like I belonged there. This actress, Dorian (not the character Dorian) Lopinto, brings us in as if we were her friends and introduces us to everyone. Maybe the kindest thing anyone had ever (has ever) done for me, and I just breezed through that studio as if I owned it. Like Norma Desmond when she's finally under the spotlight again except I had never done anything so I have no idea why the fuck I felt so at home.

I was in Llanview. Finally. (I wasn't even mad at Asa, as his earlier behavior was very much in keeping with his character.) Here I was sitting on the sofa in the Carriage House of Llanfair

(Viki Lord's estate, she wasn't working that day so I didn't get to see her, damn) with Jenny and Marco! And everything looked smaller and less fabulous, which made it all the more fabulous. And I don't remember what I said to anybody but I remember chatting and secretly positioning myself in such a way to be easily discovered by someone from casting to perhaps play a runaway, or a long-lost son, anybody, anything, I didn't want to leave. Ever. This world was so much more real to me than my own. But I do leave. And I think, "I'll be back."

Weeks later I am coming into the city with my parents and I ask them if we can drive by the studio so I can leave a thank-you gift for Dorian Lopinto. I drop off at the security desk a wrapped box of Russell Stover chocolates and a card that I have filled entirely with paragraphs of tiny, serial killer handwriting that includes all my ideas for the show, questions about upcoming storylines, and a final plea for a part, any part, on the show along with my address and phone number letting her know to get in touch with me at any time, day or night. I will be waiting. Needless to say she never responds and she is off the show a few years later. (Thank you, Dorian Lopinto.)

And high school comes and I can no longer be home by two. I start missing episodes. Watching less often. And I go to college and miss an entire year (thinking I've quit but like any good addict I am able to pick right up where I left off). I graduate, I watch occasionally and then I get sucked back in and I'm watching more frequently again (in 1992 there is a storyline that tackles homophobia in Llanview and it introduces Ryan Phillippe as Billy Douglas, a gay teenager who becomes Viki's son Joey's best friend. The entire town is involved in the story and it concludes with the AIDS quilt being shown. It was extremely groundbreaking, and it was the first time a storyline on the show had ever spoken directly to me after all these years watching it, and I was amazed at the power it had (has) over me even though I was already out and in my mid-twenties when it aired). Even just having *One Life to Live* on in the room without the volume is comforting somehow. (A Viki/Dorian episode, however, is always something I'll drop whatever I'm doing for.)

And I go to graduate school and I get a job at NYU and I plan to be a writer, want to be a writer, say I'm a writer, but don't write. And while I'm working at this office at NYU I make a friend, Evie, who also watches *One Life to Live*, has been watching as long as I have. And, then, one day, I write a letter. It's addressed to the executive producer of *One Life to Live* and in it I talk about how I grew up watching the show and that I would like to write for it. Several weeks later I get a phone call at work. Evie answers it and finds me. "It's *One Life to Live!*" They want to meet me. (It all sounds so terribly quaint now, like something out of Edith Wharton, writing a letter, waiting for a response, weeks going by, and then, a call. But it was also so exciting. A phone call now, of course, is horrible, but then, there were times when it could bring such joy.)

I return to 56 West Sixty-sixth Street. I had not been there since I dropped off my very disturbing thank-you note to Dorian Lopinto. I enter and check in at the security desk. This time, though, they have my name. An assistant comes to escort me to the executive producer. I walk through the halls oddly confident. "I told you I'd be back" I have to stop myself from saying to the first person I see. The studio is underground and it is dark and seems impossibly large for such a modest entrance. As I inhale, I drink it all in. My new stomping grounds, my colleagues, my future friends. The assistant leads me into the office of the executive producer and introduces me. I am told to take a seat. The office is made up to look like a den. Wood paneling, bookshelves, and in the middle of the room, a bar cart. The assistant begins preparing a drink for the executive producer. It is 10:00 A.M. The executive producer leans back in his chair, sucking on a cigar like a mob boss and asks me why I want to work at *One Life to Live*. (A nearby monitor shows the character Max Holden tied up to tubes in a hospital bed and all I can think is, "What happened to Max?" They are filming an episode that will not air for several weeks. I try to put this distraction out of my head.)

I go through my spiel. How much I love the show, blah blah, and he listens. And then, right there, he offers me a job. He tells me I would be working as a production assistant. That the hours would be long and hard and that I would be working for very little pay. And I ask how long before I would become a writer on the show. And he tells me there's no guarantee I would ever become a writer. That we would have to see how it goes. And I watch his assistant clear his glass and empty his ashtray and I say "no, thank you." I get up and I walk back through the studio. And I see Viki on the Llanfair set and I can't tell who she's talking to, a director maybe, and I look as long as I can until it's time for me to exit back up the stairs and out of the building.

Four years later and I am working as a bellman. I have not been paid as a writer, I have not worked as a writer, I am no closer to anything than I was that day in that office. And I am twenty-eight and I have a terrifying thought: what if that was my one chance, but I didn't recognize it and now it was too late? If I had taken that job I would surely be a writer on the show by now. I would have proven myself. I would have a career. A life. Who did I think I was?

But it wasn't my one chance. And I do get a career. The one I had always hoped for. And I keep watching *One Life to Live*. Months pass and I don't see it but still I keep up. If I'm home for the holidays, I'll turn it on and my mother will walk by the TV and notice Viki and say "she's still on?" My mother, who never watched the show, but from so many years of my watching she can't help recognizing the characters.

Years and years go by and fewer people watch soap operas and they start getting canceled. *As the World Turns*, *The Guiding Light*, and then, on the same day, *All My Children* and *One Life to Live*. I am in the writers' room of the TV show I work on when I discover this.

The final episode of the show comes, but they don't re-solve anything because they have hopes that it will continue online. And it does. Limping along in this new form for a few months, a shadow of its previous self, before it disappears completely. Unnoticed, unfinished.

And I am in the kitchen. My TV on the table. My egg sand-wich.

I watched it for thirty-three years, waiting to see how every-thing ends. And after all that, I never get to. A story should have an ending.

I DON'T FEEL WELL

I go to St. Mel's grammar school in Flushing, Queens, a few blocks from my house. My mother walks me there on my first day, and, like most gay seven-year-olds, I cry hysterically when she leaves.

We start each morning at school by standing next to our desks and reciting the Pledge of Allegiance. During these first few days, standing next to my desk, hand over my heart, I would become overwhelmed with one thought—"I've got to get the fuck out of here." The second we sat down, before the teacher had time to even start the lesson, I would approach her desk (it was only female teachers, this was the '70s) and say "I don't feel well," and she would immediately send me to the vice principal's office, who would then call my mother and have her come pick me up.

This went on about once a week for a year or so. A stomachache, a headache, a sore throat, I would rotate them the way you would meals you cook for dinner. When I was in the second grade, after God knows how many phone calls from the vice principal, my mother refused to pick me up. She had had it. "He's faking," she tells the vice principal. The vice principal then looks at me and asks, "Are you faking?" Are you out of your fucking mind? "No, I don't feel well." "He's sick, you have to come get him" and with that she hangs up. Everything's going to be okay, I say to myself, everything's going to be just fine. But I couldn't help but think I should have spaced these out a bit better. I'd really been pushing my luck lately. (The perverse thing was that my sister Maria frequently *did* get sick and refused to stay home from school, she said she didn't want to miss a thing, the twisted fuck. My mother practically had to beg her not to go. I, on the other hand, had been seemingly immune to everything—no chickenpox, no flu, no ear infections. And Maria got them all. When she had pink eye, I took the towel she used and for days rubbed it all over my face, practically shoving it into my eye sockets. I would've eaten it if I could've gotten it down. Nothing. This was my earliest illustration of irony.) And now, just like that, my mother was there in the vice principal's office and she pulls me into the hallway.

"Here," she says shoving two baby aspirin into my palm. "Take these." Oh, God, she was planning on leaving me here!

"I'm sick," I say.

"There's nothing wrong with you, you're not coming home."

Lady, you don't want to go up against me. "I'm REALLY sick."

"Get back in that classroom!"

I'm not going to lie, part of me was impressed that I'd driven my mother right up to the edge and I could see she was going to be a formidable adversary. I was even a little excited for the challenge. Up until then it had almost been too easy. Finally, I was playing tennis with someone who could hit the ball back. And right then, in that grammar school hallway, I gave the performance of my life. I would've dropped dead right there in front of her before I set one foot back in that classroom. I had cramps, I was shaking, I couldn't breathe, I did everything but spin my head around 360 degrees and throw up pea soup. The vice principal came out of her office and saw my 11 o'clock number and insisted my mother take me home. My mother gave me a look as if to say "you may have won the battle . . ." and ten minutes later I was safely in bed watching *I Love Lucy*. Still, I knew something had shifted that day and I couldn't help but feel a bit uneasy. I was going to have to be even more clever the next time.

There were a few more attempts to stay home that were thwarted by my mother. Before I even get the words "I don't feel—" out of my mouth she says "you're going to school" and she fucking means it. And then, just as I was losing hope, something incredible happened. I actually got sick. A terrible flu. Night sweats, fever, the works. I was in heaven. "So this is what it's like to be sick," I thought. I loved it. I became an eight-year-old martyr, the role I was born to play. "If it's not too much trouble just a little orange juice, please. No pulp." "Can you change the TV to *The Flintstones* and make it just a little louder but not too loud?" "Perhaps we should communicate on a notepad from now on so I can rest my throat." There was no mistaking I was ill and I immediately knew this was something I could use to my advantage. Maybe he *hasn't* been faking, my mother was no doubt beginning to think. "Remember when I said I didn't feel well last week?" I said to her. "I think it was *this* coming on. Maybe if I had stayed home it wouldn't be so bad now. I don't blame you, though. Can you turn out the light please, it's hurting my eyes."

I would occasionally leave my room to pad over to the bathroom or kitchen and then, overcome with fatigue, immediately take to my bed like Blanche DuBois. This went on for about a week. And then, like Mimi in *Rent*, my fever broke. My mother started talking about when I would be returning to school. Perhaps even tomorrow. Tomorrow? I was still quite sick I assured her and we were far from even beginning to discuss when, or if, I would be returning to school. I loved my new spa-like existence of lounging all day and breakfasts in bed and I was not about to give it up. Besides, this kind of illness at least deserved a one-week recovery period just to be safe, didn't it? The thought of returning to school was almost too much to bear. The longer I stayed away the more impossible the idea of ever returning became. My mother, still feeling a bit bad about all the times she didn't believe me and allowing that some of those times I most likely *was* sick, let me stay home a little longer. Every day she would ask how I was feeling and I would stare her down and answer flatly, "the same." But my fever was long gone and I again looked like my normal self. I could see my mother was reaching the end of her patience, but I refused to say I was feeling any better. "I get dizzy when I stand up," I told her, realizing I needed to escalate things. And she wasn't absolutely certain that I was lying, so she had no choice but to believe me. She even became concerned, as did my father, when I showed no signs of getting better.

"We're going to have to take him back to the doctor," he said. A thrill rushed through me. Yes, more doctors! It was around this point that I started to convince myself that maybe I *was* still sick. It made my performance even that much more convincing. And when they took me back to my doctor he couldn't find anything wrong with me. But he did believe me. And why wouldn't he? At this point I did, too. He then recommended my parents take me to a specialist. A specialist?! How exciting! I'd never been to a specialist before! My parents, now both worried, make an appointment for me to see this new doctor. And I stand in his office and he tells me to close my eyes and I fall back, dizzy, almost onto the ground.

"What just happened?" I ask, dramatically.

"This isn't good," he says.

"What's wrong with him?" my mother asks.

"Seemingly nothing," he tells her. "We'll have to take some tests. He might have to spend a night in the hospital."

A hospital?! This was only getting better! I continued my role as the reluctant star attraction of the family. "I'm sorry I don't feel well."

"It's not your fault," my mother replies.

I imagined myself becoming a bedridden invalid like Barbara Stanwyck in *Sorry, Wrong Number*. (Google it.) *Was* there really something wrong with me? The line between fantasy and reality was so blurred that I could no longer tell the difference. I was both cult leader *and* cult member, literally brainwashing myself. After a round of tests and still nothing I was starting to feel like there was no way out of this corner I had painted myself into short of being institutionalized. (This was before there was such a thing as chronic pain or Epstein-Barr or any other impossible-to-diagnose disease I would have happily latched on to for months.) And I could see in my mother's eyes she was starting to have some doubts. "Could this whole time he possibly have been . . ."

I only had one option left.

"I think I maybe feel a bit better today."

"Do you?" my mother responded. And it was like in that moment we had made a silent little pact, the two of us. I was going to get better—my illness departing as mysteriously as it had arrived, and she was going to let me stay home on occasion. (And this is exactly what happens. I return to school and after a few weeks the vice principal calls. "Gary's not feeling well." And she picks me up, no questions asked, and I would feel better a day or two later, both of us honoring our unspoken agreement. A détente had been reached. This goes on for years.)

But she could never be certain what had happened those weeks when no one knew what was wrong with me. Not wanting to believe I could possibly have been that devious. And, if I had been, there was no knowing what I was truly capable of. Even I didn't know.

I never wavered, I never changed my story. I never for one second said I hadn't been sick. Until now.

TIM

I see him for the first time from the library. I am procrasti-
nating studying and stare out the window (the '80s equivalent
of scrolling Instagram) when I see him go by. Tall and athletic
with glasses and blond wavy hair wearing a yellow oxford
Tommy Hilfiger shirt. My eyes follow him as he disappears out
into the student quad. I am a sophomore and have not told a
living soul yet that I am gay. He will be the first. But I won't see
him again for days. Who was this person? How would I find
out? (Today it would literally take two minutes to determine
who he was, who all his friends were, and what he looked like
in little to no clothing, and I could find out who I knew who
followed him, who had dated him, slept with him, everything I
could possibly want to know without getting up from my chair.
But in the '80s you had to be fucking Hercule Poirot. Searching

for clues. The trail of bread crumbs that would lead me back to him.)

When I finally do see him again I am walking to lunch with a friend. I think I say something to my friend like "Hey, do you know who that is I think he's in a class of mine anyway it doesn't matter I don't care I thought I knew him whatever" so as not to give away that I'm gay. I think I only admitted it fully to myself when I see him that first time out the library window. I am nineteen, almost twenty. What sad, wasted, tragic, little teenage years I had, pining for TV stars like Gregory Harrison and Mark Harmon (you can't believe what he used to look like), never having been kissed, never even having held hands with anyone, and now, a man, kind of, and, well, here we are. No wonder gay people do drugs and dance all night with their shirts off until they're fifty. My friend says she doesn't know who he is. I respond, "Who? Oh, *that* guy? No, I don't care, anyway why are we still talking about him?" But then someone else joins us and she asks him and this person does know him or something like that and I think that's when I find out his name is Tim (this person cannot 100 percent confirm the name is correct) and then more days go by. It actually makes me sick to my stomach to think how long it took me to finally speak to him from that first moment I saw him. Yellow Tommy Hilfiger shirt. Wavy blond hair. And thought of nothing else since. (Did I even know he was gay? I don't know, I barely knew I was. But yes, yes, I did, in that second from that library window I knew everything.)

Weeks go by. Information slowly drips in. Tim (confirmed).

Senior (an older man!). History major or some other useless subject. Until, one day, we meet. Through a friend, the way that you meet all people in college. I pretend like yes I possibly have seen him around campus before. "You look familiar, but there are so many people, who can be sure, really." He is friendly and bright with a beautiful smile and a voice that I can still hear. And we talk for five minutes or an hour who knows but every word, every gesture is endlessly turned over and analyzed the moment he is gone. But I have no way to determine what anything means. I have done nothing but watch TV for nineteen years. So much is new now that I'm in college on Long Island. Everything I have, everything I know, can be measured in months. My first real friendship does not happen until I'm eighteen. I know so little about this world I find myself in. I am E.T. but in a more attractive package.

So I wait. To see him again. Do I go to class during this time? Do I study? Do I write papers and take exams? I must but I don't recall. It seems like there was only this. And we have become friends. Suddenly, quickly. And can now plan meetings as opposed to leaving them to happenstance. I don't know if we are flirting. I don't know anything. We bond over nonsense, each basic thing we have in common a cause for uncorking champagne ("I like the beach, too!"). He talks to me about politics (he reads newspapers!) and how after graduation he wants to volunteer somewhere like the Peace Corps. "Yes, I do, too," I respond quickly. He could've said he wanted to strangle another student just for kicks and I would've gladly given him my belt to do it, so desperate was I to be his friend. Then, after a few weeks of God knows whatever *this* was, he asks me if I want to see a foreign film with him that will be screening in the library that weekend. I answer yes with the kind of naked enthusiasm usually reserved for lottery winners. The movie is *Das Boot*, a German film set aboard a submarine during World War II. Which is somehow both the best and worst possible thing we could be seeing. Years later I'll realize this will be my first date.

Before the film, Tim and I get dinner together at the cafeteria. One of those horrible buffets that cause most freshmen to gain fifteen pounds because they haven't learned how to regulate their eating without a parent standing by to criticize them. Luckily, I stay the same weight, already developing the kind of obnoxious tastes that will serve me well later in life. Fantasizing about a charming bistro in Paris while my contemporaries ladle puddles of gray meat into paper bowls. Tim and I sit at a cozy table for forty as other students with their tray-filled sludge come and go around us. We are a merry band of two, picking at salads (iceberg lettuce, couldn't you just die?) and talking with great importance about subjects we don't understand (at least *I* don't, he was a Fulbright scholar, that comes up a lot). And it's like two things are happening at once. What's on the surface, the banal meal we share that everyone else is seeing. And what is just underneath. A psychosexual drama of unspoken words and furtive glances.

After dinner we walk across the unispan (a hideous bridge-like structure that hovers over Hempstead Turnpike and connects the two parts of campus) together to the library and we might as well be strolling along the Seine on a starry June night. Once at the library we find our seats, and now, sitting here in the dark, my heart pounding like a jackhammer, this drab concrete slab has suddenly become the most sexually arousing place on earth. The film begins, and seeing Nazis trapped helpless in confined quarters for long periods of time takes on a charge I'm not sure was originally intended. As Tim and I sit there, watching, something incredible happens—he shifts in his seat and his knee is now ever so slightly touching my knee. I do not move my knee. I am frozen, too afraid to even breathe. Is this an accident? Do knees sometimes touch in movies and I just don't know? Has all of this just been happening in my head these many weeks? This tortured, unspoken courtship that has moved at a pace more glacial than anything Jane Austen had ever written? Am I losing my mind?? I am unraveling, unspooling, coming undone, my heart now beating so fast I fear for my life. And then he puts his hand on his knee and one finger, oh so barely, is resting on my knee. And I know now, for the first time, that this has *not* all been in my head, this has all been so very real. And I put a hand on my knee and one finger oh so barely touches his. And he presses his finger into mine and I return the pressure ever so slightly. It is an erotically charged moment that not even Anaïs Nin could imagine. We sit there watching the movie like that, our knees leaning into each other, our fingers lightly touching, for over three hours. And I could have sat there for a hundred.

When the movie ends we walk back to the parking lot together. We discuss the film. Well, he does. I was not able to concentrate on the screen. Were we not going to talk about the astonishing thing that had just transpired between us? And how would you even begin to talk about that? He is older, he is wiser, I will wait for his cues, I will let him make the first move. And I drive him back to his dorm room in my Dodge Colt. It is pouring out. God is crying because he can't believe I am taking so long to make this happen. And in my car parked outside of his dorm room I realize he is not going to say anything. And I do. I think I open my mouth and don't stop speaking for at least an hour. Delivering an aria that has been delivered by gay men across the centuries. "I don't know, this feeling, what does it mean, I'm not sure if I am . . ." You know the rest. He then opens up to me. And we talk and we talk. And I tell him I need some time. This is all so new. Tim says he understands, we will take it slowly, and I tell him I can't promise when I will be ready. I walk him into the lobby of his dorm building. Our long, thick hair matted from the rain (if there's anything sexier than young people wet I haven't seen it). He promises to be patient. My resolve lasts as far as the elevator. Practically devouring him as soon as the doors close behind us. It is much easier than I had anticipated and my first thought is "Why have I made such a big fucking deal out of this for twenty years?"

I spend that night in his dorm room. He has a single. So luxurious—it's the college equivalent of finding yourself waking up in a Park Avenue penthouse. ("All this is *ours*?" as I roll around the futon and gaze at his dresser and one window.)

And we begin a secret affair that within twelve hours I want to shout from the rooftops. ("I'm going to be with him forever!" "I don't care who knows!" "FUCK EVERYONE!") And my friends become his and his mine. We are close in the way men in college can become instantly close in the '80s without arousing suspicion. "Oh, yes, Gary and Tim are completely inseparable now and they didn't know each other yesterday. We accept this no questions asked." I am flying. Heroin wishes it felt this good. The things I cared about mere days ago mean nothing. There is only Tim. I am every song from every musical. I am bursting all the time. How can people still think this is the same Gary? My parents, my sister, friends, all idiots. Wake up! I am a different person now! Slowly Tim and I tell our friends. One by one letting them into our tiny circle. Each new person that knows sends a thrill like no other through me. So guarded is this information it feels as though I am holding the nuclear codes. "You have to swear not to tell anyone what we are about to tell you. Close the door and make sure it's locked. We need you to stay calm because this is *that* big!" I was finally the star of my own movie and it was fucking amazing. I was in love. I had a secret. I was gorgeous. The fact that Tim was also the nephew of the president of the university only added that much more frisson to the proceedings.

Months go by and I am happier than I have ever been. Dinners at Pizza Hut, movies at the Roosevelt Field Mall, nights in his single dorm room at Tower B, literally a fairy tale.

I wasn't aware that the second I finally tell someone I am gay how much easier everything will then get. I smile, I look up, I sleep. (I, of course, also immediately know: I have to start working out. This is the deal with the devil we make as gay men. As Debbie Allen would say, "Fame costs, and right here's where you start paying.") We tell more and more people, one at a time. Each new conversation given the dramatic heft of a Eugene O'Neill play. And lasting as long as one, too.

After so many years of nothing, how delicious to be the center of so much everything. All of our friends loved and accepted us, of course, and celebrated us accordingly. We were Tony and Maria. We were Heathcliff and Cathy. We were Luke and Laura. It was the heady days of being the "It Couple" of Hofstra University for one semester in the mid-'80s among a dozen people. And then, just like that, it all came tumbling down.

He wanted to talk to me, he said. Had I done something wrong? No, no, everything was fine, I assured myself. Going over every interaction we'd had the last few days like a court transcript. Nothing was amiss. Then why did I feel such dread?

"It's like we both want different things," he said.

NO WE DON'T, I WANT WHAT YOU WANT!

"What do you mean?" I ask.

And he tells me we haven't talked about politics and the situation in Central America that much lately, and that's important to him (the Fulbright scholar stuff comes up again here, but we are only at Hofstra University so let's get a fucking grip, shall we?). And I'm thinking, "Did we ever talk about the situation in Central America?" And I remember he did. He talked about a lot of things. I listened. Pretending to find them interesting because he was cute. That's what people do! I tell him as much. "I don't really care about all that, I care about you." And he tells me I misled him. I had never even *led* anyone before much less *mis*-led them. He thinks we should have some time apart and doesn't want to see me for a while. I should state right here for the record I was much better-looking than he was, and on those grounds alone this was ludicrous. "Because I don't want to talk about Central America?! I'm nineteen!" (Okay, I'm twenty.) And I start replaying in my mind all the conversations we had and realize he did most of the talking. And that he was really fucking boring. Or maybe I'm telling myself this. But I don't remember laughing a lot. I am devastated, though. And, Scarlett O'Hara–like, I vow as God as my witness no one will ever break up with me again.

But what I am to discover in my heartbreak is as much drama surrounded me when I was telling people I was in a secret relationship, that much more surrounds me now that I am part of an ugly breakup. I no longer have to share the spotlight with a towheaded, pseudointellectual blowhard. I am the gorgeous, wronged party, the center of everything, the leading lady. A tragic figure of both pity and lust. And I fucking love it. I have watched *One Life to Live* long enough to know how to wring every last drop out of this.

It's not long before Tim has another boyfriend he's parading around campus. Some little slut he can talk about Nicaraguan dictators with no doubt. And I meet somebody else soon after, too. Things happen very quickly once you start to come out. Toppling down walls overnight you spent decades building.

We only talk a few more times after that. So odd you can be so close to someone and then instantly become strangers. Nothing more than what he was on that first day in the library. Another anonymous man I see while looking through a window.

WALDBAUM'S

When I am sixteen it is time to apply for an after-school job. This is something that is quite common among children of those who are not wealthy or celebrities. We get jobs so we can buy stuff—sneakers, jeans—and save for college. (In Los Angeles I see many children of the affluent getting after-school jobs so they can learn responsibility and what it means to have to earn your own money. I don't believe this works. If I knew my parents were rich, I would have waltzed into every job like I owned the place. "I have to leave early, you know what, on second thought, I'm leaving now." You can't learn the value of money unless you actually really need that fucking money.) It never even crossed my mind that I wouldn't be working once I hit sixteen. I didn't know anyone who didn't have an after-school job. I lived in Queens not Monte Carlo.

If you wanted a car, or to go to the movies, or to get anything, you needed a job. My older sister, Maria, started at McDonald's when she was fifteen. That's not even legal. There were weeks I think she worked over forty hours. But nobody cared, it was the '70s. People were still smoking. (My mother putting ashtrays out whenever company would visit. What was more fabulous than my godmother, Pat, sitting on our couch popping Planters peanuts and dragging on a Virginia Slims? Nothing. I miss people smoking. Sometimes I go to Europe just to inhale the fumes.)

A job also seemed extremely grown-up. I felt Maria had seen more of the world just by working four blocks away than I ever would. It was only the McDonald's on Francis Lewis Boulevard, but to me she might as well have been trading stocks on Wall Street.

My first interview is at the McDonald's where my sister works. And I do not get the job. How was this possible? If my sister had gone to Yale University, as her sibling I would have been given more of an advantage than I ever was at McDonald's. To this day I still can't figure out what the fuck I must have said in that interview to make them go "no, not for us." They loved my sister. Pretty, smart, and personable, adored by all, she was their star cashier. That's how much they must have hated me. I have to admit I was thrown. I was a very good-looking child. You would have had to be insane not to want to put me in a powder-blue polyester uniform (that's what it was then) and slap me in front of the public. I remember even my mother being blindsided when I didn't get the job. "What did you say to them??" I wondered if this was going to be a harbinger for the rest of my working life. If McDonald's was setting the bar too high, what was lower? Prostitute? The truth was I didn't even want to work there. My sister was an icon at the Francis Lewis Boulevard McDonald's and I would never have been able to live up to those lofty expectations. I wanted to forge my own path. Fortunately, my sister (Maria is my gateway to most everything throughout my childhood) has a friend who knows someone who works at Waldbaum's supermarket (one in a chain) and can get me an interview. (You know how they say you need to know someone if you want to work in Hollywood? Well, you need to know someone if you want to work at the Waldbaum's in Flushing, too.)

I meet with the store manager in his office basement. He's very professional, and kind, and has a mustache. I get the job and am given my polyester Waldbaum's smock. Everything is polyester then. I am going to be a cashier.

It takes me about an hour into my first shift to become drunk with power. It is my job to ring in every item. There are no barcodes to scan and the cash registers are not computerized. It's like having grown up in a time when we rode horses instead of cars. Little stickers are put on every item with a pricing gun. And if these little stickers fell off you had no way of knowing how much the item cost without shouting "I need a price!" to the bookkeeper, who would then come over with an actual book and look up said price. This could take a while and slow your line down considerably. I liked to keep things moving so would often make up the prices. The trick was to always pick a price that you know is going to be lower than the actual one. If a can of beans was usually around sixty-nine cents I would punch in forty-nine cents. This way most people would never question me—and when they did question me, so help them God. "Are you sure that's the right price?" "Oh, you think I'm overcharging you? Let me check. I NEED A PRICE!" Then I would let everything come to a grinding halt as I waited for the bookkeeper to come over and check the price. If the next person in line would ask what the holdup was, I would explain that I was waiting for a price because this lady thinks I charged her too much for a can of beans. When the price would inevitably come back as *higher* than I charged them, well, I'm smiling right now just thinking about it. "You were correct it *was* the wrong price," and then I would go on to punch in the extra twenty cents they owed. Nobody fucked with me when I was on the register.

I became a popular cashier. Many regular customers only going to my line. I moved quickly, I knew how to pack bags. (Each one its own little puzzle. To this day I can't go into a market and not pack my own groceries.) I was charming, Waldbaum's was my cocktail party, and I was its host. Also, by this time, many customers realized that if anything didn't have a price I always made up a lower one. And I took coupons that had expired. Or gave the sale price on items that were no longer on sale. In short, I did whatever the hell I wanted.

And if I liked you, or you were particularly kind to me, or complimented my looks, I would give you roughly every third item free. I'm sure most of the customers thought I was in some way mentally challenged, how could they know I saw myself as a kind of Robin Hood of Flushing. Taking from Waldbaum's and giving a little back to the people I thought it would help the most. I remember one woman who was quite pretty with two small sons and I could tell money was a struggle, there appeared to be no husband in the picture, so whenever she had a roast or a steak or a turkey I just put it through without ringing it up. I knew she was aware of what I was doing when she started coming up to my register with more expensive cuts of meat.

There was really no way I could be found out. There were no cameras, there were no computers, and nobody was all that invested. I would actually feel bad on the rare occasions I would charge a customer for everything they had bought. I liked the thought of some old lady arriving back at her apartment, unpacking her groceries, going over her receipt, and realizing she hadn't been charged for a gallon of ice cream. It's on me.

The store stayed open late on Thursday and Friday nights. (My father taping *Knots Landing* for me on those Thursday evenings I am not at home, one week—a particularly pivotal episode, Valene's twins had been stolen, she was told they had died, and Karen was on the verge of discovering everything—he accidentally forgets and it sends me into a tailspin I am only recently coming out of.) After the store closes at night we would do something known as leveling. Which is basically straightening up the shelves. During this time, we would strut through the aisles behaving as if we were in a lawless Old West town. We stuck our fists into bags of candy, made sandwiches, huffed whipped cream, ate from cereal boxes. None of us thought of this as stealing. I brought home at least fifty dollars' worth of magazines a week. Rifling through the racks like it was my own personal library. These were just perks of the job. If this happened today I would likely be put in prison, my future most certainly ruined. Then, it was just shit you did. It was a different world. Pregnant women smoked, we drove without seat belts, every day was Russian roulette.

I enjoy being part of the workforce. I take on as many shifts as I can. Spending my money on theater tickets and Italian shoes—like most sixteen-year-old boys. I know everyone who works at the store, I know everyone who comes into the store, and everyone knows me. I feel accepted in a way that I never have at school. And it feels good.

I work at Waldbaum's for the rest of high school. I go to college and I continue to work, but just on Saturdays. "They like you there," my mother tells me, "you'd be a fool to give up that job." She's probably still troubled by my failed McDonald's interview, and who could blame her. For all we know there might not *be* another job.

When I am nineteen I go to Oxford to study drama for the summer and while I am away the store closes. When I come back I am reassigned to a different one. (I was in a union, steady raises, double time on Sundays, paid holidays—take that, Maria!) This new Waldbaum's is only a few blocks away from the old one but may as well be on the moon. I don't know anyone—the customers, the other employees, the store itself is different. I'm different, I realize. Two others from my old store are also transferred here. We reminisce like war vets. I hear about the last days of our store, the aisles emptying, customers saying goodbye, and I wish I had been there. Because I would have liked to have had the chance to acknowledge it for what it was. A chapter of my life that has now ended. I work there only one or two Saturdays more. Always know when to leave the party.

LETTER TO MY YOUNGER SELF

Dear Gary,

I have so much to tell you! I don't even know where to begin, girl! Oh, right, let's start there. You're gay. It's not a big deal so just relax, I can already see you freaking the fuck out. And spare yourself all the "maybe I am, maybe I'm not" bullshit. You're gay. Trust me. And not like a little gay. A lot. If the Kinsey scale went to 10 it still wouldn't be high enough. I've literally just saved you at least a decade of torturing yourself over this. Please use the extra time to learn another language. You will get sick of telling people when you travel that you only speak English and vow to take a French course once you get home but never will.

I would also suggest hitting the gym the second you turn fifteen and hitting it hard. There is no minimizing the importance a good body is going to play in your future so why not start as early as possible. And you will never think your body is good enough. This is completely common. It is called body dysmorphia and every gay man has it. But know that your body from the ages of eighteen to twenty-five is going to be the closest you will ever come to God. Please enjoy it. And stop fantasizing that every man who smiles at you is going to become your boyfriend and you're going to immediately move in together. You're not a lesbian. Relax. Smile back. Flirt. Also, if you ask someone out and they say "no" it's not the end of the fucking world. You really need to chill out about this. Don't always wait for someone to come up and talk to you. Standing around bars like you're wearing a poodle skirt at a sock hop. Go up to people. Ask their name. Go home with them. Don't call them the next day. YOU be the jerk.

And you know how you think you're not good at sports? You're actually not bad. Concentrate more on the gay sports, though. We obviously like swimming, do more of that, get better at that. Look good in a Speedo. Everything else will fall into place. Thank Mom and Dad for the tennis lessons and stop complaining about them. Tennis, swimming, running, these are all sexy sports. Do more of them. Oh, God, don't tan as much as you do!

This is very important!! Do not lay in the sun (lie in the sun? You never learn which is correct) eight hours a day every summer for your entire twenties. You will think this looks good at the time but when you see pictures years later you will realize how fucking crazy you looked.

This is also very important. Never take the first table they offer you in a restaurant. Don't even start walking with the host until you know where you're going. "What table were you thinking of giving us?" always lets them know you mean business right off the bat. Never sit by the door, near a waiter station, or across from the bathroom. Always take the seat facing out to the room. If there is a booth available you definitely want that. Never wait more than ten minutes without bombarding the host with questions about your table. The host will always be another gay man. You need to play this very carefully. Gay men with even the tiniest bit of power abuse it with a sick relish. (If Hitler were gay we'd all be speaking German.) Let him know that you are another gay man who is not in competition with him, nor do you see yourself as better than he in any way. Humble yourself to him. Compliment his hair or horrible too-tight shirt. You must somehow win him over. Only then will you have a chance at a decent table with minimal waiting. Learn his name, become his friend. Kiss him on both cheeks your next time at the restaurant. Pretend you are interested in how he has been since the last time you saw him. His interests, his goals for the future. You must keep up this charade as long as this person is host. Once they are gone from this job they no longer exist to you. Free that space in your brain for the next host you will need to curry favor with.

Hotels are just as tricky. All men who work behind the front desk at hotels are also gay. Use similar methods as with restaurant hosts to ensure you get the best possible room. Know that you will never be happy at any hotel in the world unless you have been given an upgrade. An upgrade is something you always want. It is perhaps even more important than the trip itself. You should plant the seeds for this as soon as your reservation has been booked. If you are staying in a hotel near the water and your room isn't directly facing the water, know that means something has gone terribly wrong with your life. If they offer a water view or city view and you end up with city view you might as well go home. You never want an inner courtyard view. You will hear people at all hours of the day, their voices bouncing off the walls like Ping-Pong balls. This will torture you even if you hear no voices after the first five minutes of arriving in your room. There will always be the possibility of it starting up again. Which is somehow even worse. If you complain enough 90 percent of the time you will get aforementioned upgrade. Only then will you begin to relax and truly enjoy your vacation.

Know that traveling by air will always be a torture and mentally prepare yourself accordingly. Always remember that you *think* you like sitting in the first row but then get annoyed by the chitchat between male flight attendants (also all gay) that inevitably occurs during the time of the flight when most people are sleeping. When you shush them it will not go over well, especially after 9/11. You will employ more passive-aggressive tactics such as waking with a start, as if you don't know where this noise is coming from, and when passing them on your way to the bathroom, shooting a look that lets them know their gibbering as they share an *Us* magazine is what got you up. This may not solve anything but will give you a certain amount of satisfaction. You will derive much satisfaction in later life simply by shooting looks at people.

And most important, stop wanting to be older!! It's perverse! Enjoy every minute of every day in your young body! Touch your skin. Marvel at its smoothness. And how it instantly snaps back when you pull it. Stare at your hair in the mirror. It is almost black. Stop wanting it to be lighter. It is thick and dark and perfect. And don't put Sun-In in it! It turns your hair orange! When you get to high school try talking to people. Make a friend. Don't shut down for four years. Try to experience something. It will be difficult, I know. I couldn't do it or else I wouldn't be writing this letter. But here's something that might help you. Teenagers are stupid. Nothing more than insecure little narcissists covered in zits. Find one or two you can hang out with to make fun of the rest of them. This is all that teenagers do anyway. You just need a person. To sit with at lunch. To go to a movie with. To call on the phone. That would've been nice, I think. I'd like that for you.

Let's see, what else? Don't go into debt over clothes. Hug your dogs while you have them. Know that you can skip most anything. You will fall in love eventually. Remember that.

Also, the things you like aren't weird. Don't worry about being normal. It's an awful thing to aspire to.

I don't want you to think it's all bad now, though. There's *A Chorus Line*. And *The Carol Burnett Show*. Your sister. Fresh bagels on Sundays. So much is wonderful.

xo, G

SAKS FIFTH AVENUE

In my second year of college I get what will be the first of many part-time salesman jobs. I work the floor of the menswear department at Saks. Not the one on Fifth Avenue, though. The one on Long Island in Garden City. Long Island has many stores and restaurants that are pale imitations of their Manhattan counterparts. Yet Long Islanders somehow think they are of equivalent value. Not unlike the Canadian that insists Toronto is just as vibrant and cosmopolitan as New York City. Yes, Toronto is exactly like New York City if New York City were a suburb of Boston. As stores go it's nice enough. But the way they go on about it in Garden City you'd think it was the fucking Hermitage Museum.

In my mind Garden City will always be famous for one thing and one thing only. It is the home of Susan Lucci. Star of

All My Children and national treasure. My first question after I get the job is "Does Susan Lucci shop here?" The answer is "Of course she fucking does." The store would be informed before each of Ms. Lucci's visits and a military-like operation would then go into effect, much as I imagine would be expected for arriving heads of state or Beyoncé. Phones would ring, whispers would pass from employee to employee, creating an impromptu dance routine that was almost haunting in its silence. "She's coming." Anticipation and tension filled the air with equal measure. I had been working at the store only a short while when the first of these visits was announced. We were instructed by our manager to straighten the department. Everyone needed to be on the floor. Nobody was on break when Susan Lucci was due to arrive. It was all hands on deck. And I had never been more excited in my life. Meeting Susan Lucci could be a real game changer for me. Now I'm not saying I thought she was going to offer me a role on *All My Children*. But I could start laying the foundation. I would charm her, flatter her, I would become "her guy." She would want to be helped only by me when she came into the store. We would gossip about the other employees and share private jokes. I would be the Truman Capote to her Babe Paley. She would eventually usher me into a world of celebrity and privilege that up until now I'd only seen in the pages of magazines. It wouldn't be long before she would introduce me to the casting director of *All My Children*. "Find something for Gary," she'd say breezily on her way to a wardrobe fitting. The other actors jealous that I was her new pet. But I'd prove I was more than just eye candy, I had real chops, too. Dominating every scene that I was in, but not too much so, always careful not to upset the balance of power in our relationship. When people would ask where Susan and I had met we both would look at each other, as if to say "Where *did* we meet?" so impossible was it to remember a time without the other. And today was going to be the first brick in that wall. All the employees stand straight at their posts ready to greet her. Every sweater freshly folded, every hanger precisely placed, every everything perfect. But, like Godot, she doesn't ever arrive. I feel cheated, angry even. "Why would she say she was coming and then not come? That's fucked up."

I'm told this happens frequently. We should treat these as emergency drills. Everyone relaxes and returns to their normal slouchy, couldn't-give-a-shit demeanor. Did Susan Lucci know her capriciousness affected hundreds of lives? I bet she did.

I become friends with one of my fellow salesmen, Brian. Brian is from Long Island and goes to a different college. He comes out to me after we've been working together a few weeks. And instead of taking this opportunity to come out in return to him, I play the part of the understanding and supportive ally. "I'm so glad you told me" "this doesn't change anything," etc. (Perhaps this would have played out differently if I were in any way attracted to him, but no dice.) I become his confidant, his shoulder to cry on, as he tells me stories from a life that I am not yet a part of. Nights out at clubs, dates gone wrong, men he meets. I absorb every bit of information like a sponge. "And then what happened? And what was that like?" Hungrily sucking the marrow out of each last detail. But Brian never questions me about myself, never pushes me, even though it couldn't be more apparent I was gay if my head were a disco ball.

One day Brian asks me if I want to go out to a bar with him. It's a gay bar. On Long Island. I didn't even know they had them on Long Island. In a magnanimous show of acceptance of his lifestyle I say yes.

I drive to a strip mall a few towns over. I meet him out front. The first thing I am struck by when I enter is how ordinary everything is. Just people drinking, having a good time. I don't know what I was expecting. Caligula's Rome, maybe. Definitely more than guys in chinos sipping beer. I wasn't much of a drinker, so afraid was I of doing anything that would lower my inhibition, allowing me to stare too long, say something I couldn't take back—be, in any way, me. I conducted myself in every social situation with the control and composure of Jackie Kennedy at JFK's funeral.

We stay for a little while. Chat. He knows people. And the big moment I'm expecting never comes. Nobody welcomes me. People don't gather round, desperate to know my story, pulling it out of me, bit by bit, hanging on my every word. I don't get twirled onto the dance floor or lifted aloft or begrudgingly dragged into the spotlight to be applauded. Celebrated. Embraced. It's just a regular Thursday night at a strip mall bar in Farmingdale. I don't tell Brian I'm gay that evening. I don't get a phone number. I don't flirt. I don't think I even smile. I watch, I observe. I'm good at that. And then, when I've had enough, "I think I'm gonna go."

A week or so later, while I'm at work, Brian walks up to me. "She's coming." And I immediately know what he's referring to. I frantically begin to straighten the department. There is a buzz of activity all around the store. Brian tells me he has helped her pick out shirts for her husband before. "What's she like?" I ask. He thinks and then says, "What you'd expect." I expect her to get me the fuck out of here, so good! A salesgirl from another department suddenly appears, panting, "She's in cosmetics!" I take off in a mad dash for the cosmetics department, and there she is. Susan Lucci in a full-length fur coat pointing at something under a glass case. Tapping on it lightly with one perfectly manicured nail. She is completely made up and it is difficult to see her as anything other than Erica Kane, the character she has been famously playing for decades. The thought of going up to her now ridiculous.

I watch as she interacts with the older saleswoman who is helping her. A well-timed laugh, a smile, a nod, it's all flawlessly executed. And for a moment instead of Garden City, we are in Pine Valley, the fictional home of *All My Children*. And my life is the show. But I am not one of the stars. I am only an extra.

I walk back to the menswear department. And I stand there. Waiting for something to happen.

AMERICAN YOUTH HOSTELS

During the summer of my sophomore year of college I get a job leading a bicycle trip through Europe for rich New York City teenagers. It is for American Youth Hostels, an organization that puts unqualified twenty-year-olds in charge of the lives of sixteen-year-olds. We will be camping and staying in youth hostels for six weeks, carrying cooking equipment and tents on our bikes. We have no itinerary, we are to make it up as we go along, riding anywhere from thirty to a hundred miles a day. This specific trip is called Phantom Europe, and it is the only one offered that has no discernible itinerary other than we leave and depart from Paris. There are twelve kids on the trip, known in American Youth Hostels lingo as trippers. I will be co-leading the group with a woman named Brenda from

Colorado (a state I know only from John Denver songs but feel like that's enough to get it).

Brenda and I meet for the first time at the airport the day of the trip where we immediately discover neither of us speaks another language or is good with maps. (This is before GPS or anything else helpful existed.) I'm not sure why we were paired together for this uniquely challenging trip, since we both bring nothing to the table. We do agree we'd like to go to Italy, which according to the bumps we see on the map, appears to be quite hilly. I am recently twenty. She is twenty-one. These parents had to have been insane to let us take their children across the ocean with no plan, skills, or experience whatsoever. But rich people aren't normal. They're used to going without seeing their children for incredibly long stretches, sometimes even years. Middle-class families don't have the luxury of avoiding each other. Forced to all live together in small homes, often two to a room, sharing meals, watching TV together like animals. Rich families, on the other hand, checked in on each other with the same infrequency you would a friend who lived in a different city. Occasional phone calls, dinners once a month, that sort of thing.

American Youth Hostels was akin to Outward Bound, the program that leaves wealthy teenagers alone in the woods for several days, with no food or water, in order to prepare them for a life of Four Seasons and Aman Resorts. I get the job after going through a week-long training program that involves sitting in a circle and sharing the kinds of insipid things twenty-year-olds share and learning how to change a flat tire. I'm not quite sure how this prepares me for keeping alive a dozen children as we cycle blindly through the Italian Alps. I've been to Europe once before and ridden a bike around Queens when I was a kid, other than that I have nothing to offer aside from being game and attractive. Which both opens more doors than you'd think, and not as many.

We all meet at JFK, the trippers being dropped off by their parents. We exchange greetings, no one seeming particularly worried. And there are no cell phones, so after dumping their kids in the International Terminal with a bicycle and their panniers (the bags that hang off the back wheel that you store all your stuff in) it's basically "see you in six weeks."

A part of me still thinking, "Somebody's going to stop this, aren't they?" (Even my mother is skeptical. "*Who's* in charge of this again?" I explain it's totally on the up-and-up and I was lucky to have been chosen. Once she hears I had to beat out other people for the job she relaxes. This legitimizes it somehow, and I think she assumes the whole enterprise is a lot more professionally run than it actually is. "I guess they must have some kind of contingency plan that goes into effect in case anything goes wrong," she says. "I guess," I say, knowing they don't. "They must," she repeats, reassuring herself, and this being the '80s and not being able to Google anything that was the end of that.)

And suddenly Brenda and I are left in the airport with twelve teenagers, round-trip tickets to Paris (thick paper booklets then, like you were crossing on the *Titanic*), traveler's checks, and a map of Europe. We disassemble our bikes and put them into boxes so they can be put through baggage check. (I was quite handy then, I have no recollection of how I did any of this, today I can barely get the plastic off an Altoids tin.)

I use this time to size up the trippers. See if I can suss out any problem ones. So far they all appear okay. Some of the kids are really into biking, though, and seem to think we will be doing at least eighty miles a day. I was hoping to keep this on the low end of the "anywhere from thirty to a hundred miles a day" as the trip was described in the brochure. I'm picturing our riding to be very *Sound of Music* montage–like and am getting a bit nervous that several of them have something considerably more strenuous in mind. Brenda, being from Colorado and used to hiking mountains before breakfast, is only too eager to encourage us to bike as much as we possibly can each day. And I think, "Why am I doing this again?"

It's right around this time that I have started to come out of the closet. It doesn't happen all at once but plays out rather in slow motion. A roundelay of person-to-person confessionals. An event television series padded with too many episodes to tell its thin story. Before I even came out to anyone, I started dipping my toe into the water. Wandering onto the gay section of Jones Beach by "mistake." (Field six, to the left of the parking lot, keep walking, gay beaches are always a long walk. You can drop me on any coast in the world, blindfold me, spin me around, and like a homing pigeon, I will automatically find my way to the gay section.) Taking my first trip to a gay bar as the progressive friend of a gay coworker and even going for a weekend away with my college friend Anthony to a B and B in Provincetown. ("This place is crazy!")

(Anthony is my first real friend and we quickly form a close bond that is something I haven't experienced before. He is adorable, brown curly hair, teeth, khakis, and I learn how to dance from watching him. We go to the campus club, Hofstra USA, together and it might as well have been fucking Studio 54. We eat together, we take classes together, we do everything together. He is straight and I fall in love with him the way you do with your first real friend. We lose touch after graduation, I don't know why. All these years later and I still dance like Anthony did at eighteen.)

I approach each of these outings as if I'm Jane Goodall. Observing, studying, watching, pencil always at the ready. ("Drag brunch, *All About Eve*, glory holes, got it!")

I decide I want to physically challenge myself, do something that maybe doesn't seem gay. Prove something to myself. I'm not sure what exactly. But I guess I know in short order I will be out to the world, and maybe leading this bicycle trip is one last chance for me to try to be the kind of guy that other guys are. To finally be like everyone else. In any case, there's no going back now.

Once on board the plane there is a mix-up with our tickets and as a result Brenda and I both end up getting bumped into Business Class. This ruins me for the next six weeks, since the flight will now be the nicest part of the trip. I suddenly hate the people in economy. ("Can you ask them to keep it down back there, thanks.") I drink champagne as if I had been born with it fused into my hand. Already holding my glass out for a refill without breaking conversation like a pro. I'm wearing shorts and a T-shirt and I can't help feeling underdressed. Little did I know at the time I was wearing the most desirable thing possible, a twenty-year-old body. When we land in Paris I don't want to get off the plane. This is the first stage of a trip whose next stop should be a suite at the Ritz not sleeping in the dirt. I want to go on *that* trip not this one. This has been a cruel tease. Invited into a world I'm already being kicked out of. "How was the flight?" one of the kids asks me once we're in the airport. "I don't want to talk about it."

We wait at baggage claim for the boxes that contain our bikes and reassemble them right there. Our plan is to take the Métro into Paris and then start cycling to the Loire Valley, and from there who knows. Brenda rides first, in the position that is known as point, and I follow behind last, in the position known as sweep. The trippers strung between us like Christmas lights.

I like being last. I let everyone ride way ahead of me. Waiting a bit before I start pedaling so I can't see anyone else when I ride. I pretend that I am alone, that I have chosen to travel like this, with only a tent and a cook set. I stop along the way at each patisserie I pass. Cycling off the calories until it's time to stop at the next one. Imagining a life made up of mille-feuilles and pains au chocolat. Sometimes I lose track of time and fall too far behind everyone else. When I see one or two of them waiting ahead for me at some distant point I wave them on, the "I'm fine!" pastry still on my face. The first few days go by without incident. We bike, we cook, we camp. Bike, cook, camp. Then we decide to hop on a train to the South of France so we can cover ground more quickly. From there our plan is to cycle along the coast into Italy.

I find that despite myself I'm actually good at this. The kids seem to like me and I like them. Brenda and I get along well, and we're even doing an okay job. Occasionally one of the trippers would get upset if they thought we were favoring one over the other, or they didn't like what we were cooking, what their chores were, where we decided to cycle. Every day was a thousand decisions, and not everyone was happy all the time. (Now kids would text their parents, raging over each tiny injustice, but then they had to just suck it up.)

I feel my body getting stronger, my confidence rising (the tan helps), and I can no longer remember my life before this. I am capable, strong, dependable. I can fix bikes, put up a tent, cook for fourteen people with one pot and a propane burner. I fall asleep each night from exhaustion. I feel more masculine than I ever have before in my life. There are so many things I had never done out of fear. I vow to do all of them.

We cycle into Monaco along the road Princess Grace's car swerved off of. (When I'm ten I see her in *To Catch a Thief* with Cary Grant on The 4:30 Movie. It is the first time I have ever heard of the French Riviera and know instantly if Grace Kelly is there it has to be the most glamorous place on earth.) The entire country appears to be one giant Business Class. Every road, every car, every building pristine. It's like a movie set for the fanciest place on Earth. If there's a poor part of town they must keep it in Italy.

While I'm riding sweep I catch up to the tripper who has been riding in front of me, Amanda. She's had an accident, she's not hurt but her bike is badly damaged. The two of us hitchhike into town where we meet up with the rest of the group. We bring Amanda's bike to be repaired, but they are going to need two days to fix it. We all decide to stay at a youth hostel in Monte Carlo until it's finished and then continue on to Italy according to plan.

We check into the Princess Stephanie Youth Hostel, and it's literally like the nicest hotel I've ever been in. It has private rooms and a swimming pool. We are all ecstatic. Up until now we have been camping in open fields with a night at the occasional disgusting hostel. We have dinner at a café on the Riviera. Later that night there's an outdoor screening of Martin Scorsese's *New York, New York*, starring Robert De Niro and Liza Minnelli. We watch while eating ice cream, boats bobbing all around us. We spend the next day by the pool, walking around town, sipping coffees. And then it's time to pick up Amanda's bike and continue cycling. I'm not looking forward to another few weeks of shaking worms out of my sleeping bag, but these few days have been good for everyone. We have bonded. We are a group.

Before we check out of the youth hostel I notice there is a guest book and leaf through it. Flipping to the last pages I see that several of the trippers have already signed it. I read what they've written. Little notes, little letters, yearbook-style, and then I see my name. One of them has written that they all like me. But they think that I'm gay. It comes with no judgment, just a statement of fact. We think he's gay. We talk about it. We're not sure. But we think he's gay. And I feel sick. I shouldn't, I know. It's like there's nothing I can do. All the bike riding, all the camping in the world is not enough, anything I do, nothing is enough to make anyone see anything else. Was I trying not to show it, trying to pass, is that why I took this job? Maybe. I don't know. But me at my most masculine was still gay enough for an average teenager to detect it instantly. And part of me thinks no matter what you do, this is you. You can't hide it. You've never been able to hide it. I feel stupid. Embarrassed. This letter for everyone who passes through to read now. My secret made public by children in a fucking guest book. Do I take it? Who gives a fuck anymore? I'm just tired mostly at this point.

The next few days promise to be the most difficult of the trip. We're crossing a section of the Italian Alps. From there we'll go on to Pisa and through Northern Italy and back to Paris. I care a little less now about what I say, what I do, how I carry myself. If they like me, if they don't. I'm aloof. I can't tell if I'm putting walls up or taking them down. Brenda asks if I'm okay, I say yes, yes, fine. Not knowing if she's read what was written about me. Wanting to talk to someone. I should have talked to her. She was kind. (*Did* I maybe?? There's a part of me that wonders now if I did. I can't remember it, though.)

It seems like the ride uphill goes on forever. Winding round and round, higher and higher, it's impossible to know how much farther up there is to go. Hours pass, creeping slowly on our bikes, as we wind higher still. It feels like the most difficult thing I've ever done. And when I think I can't go on any longer I round one more final turn and suddenly, just like that, I'm going downhill. Picking up speed, faster and faster. And it's all so beautiful. Like flying through a postcard. A blur of color and sky. As long as it took to get to the top it takes maybe twenty minutes to reach the bottom. Gaining more speed as I get closer and closer. I see a town in the distance. Up ahead, sprinkled like crumbs, I see Brenda and the other trippers. And as I reach the town I hear something and at first I don't know what it is. Then I realize it's crying, and now I see her. An old woman dressed in black standing in the middle of the road. She bends to pick up a cat that has just been run over by a car. She cradles it in her arms, sobbing sobbing. But I don't stop. I am already too far from everyone else.

STEVEN CARRINGTON

I watch an extraordinary amount of TV as a kid. My actual life is a blip. Snippets that occur between favorite programs. School is an unwelcome interruption from the more pressing matters of sitcom reruns and game shows. We are not allowed to watch TV during dinner, but aside from those excruciating ten minutes I'm pretty much free to sit in front of it every other hour of the day. I get up to TV, I come home to TV, and I go to bed to TV. *Name That Tune*–like, I could tell you what any episode of *The Brady Bunch* was within the first seconds. Saturday mornings I'd be up at seven and sit there watching for twelve hours. There weren't that many channels then, so you'd be forced to see a lot of old movies in the afternoons. And parents didn't monitor what their kids watched in the '70s, so you saw everything. I watched Maude get an abortion when I was six. Nobody cared. Not that I knew exactly what was happening, but I got the gist (Baby no baby). I learned to love Hitchcock and Bette Davis before I entered first grade. I'd watch *Wait Until Dark* on The 4:30 Movie where an impossibly chic, blind Audrey Hepburn was terrorized in her Manhattan apartment by Alan Arkin of all people. Pluckily smashing lightbulbs to even the playing field while he ransacks the place looking for a child's doll stuffed with heroin.

Another day it was a hysterical Tippi Hedren swatting birds off her face. Or Joan Crawford baking pies for her ingrate daughter. Ingrid Bergman slowly being driven insane by Charles Boyer fucking with the lights. I watched it all.

I loved Mary and Rhoda. Carol Burnett. Laverne and Shirley. Lucy. Worshipfully watching each show with the devotion of a Sea Org–level Scientologist.

And then there was Cher. I didn't know why I fixated on her at the time, inexplicably drawn to her from the age of five when *The Sonny and Cher Show* first began. Sitting an inch away from the TV, wanting to get as close to her as possible. She sang, she danced, she was funny, she wore incredible outfits, and she didn't give a fuck. There was no one like Cher. She single-handedly represented everyone who was outside the norm. Everyone who didn't fit in. I already knew I was different and here was Cher to let me know how fabulous being different could be. I belonged somewhere, even if it was only for an hour a week.

Today kids have thousands of role models. And a Google

search will instantly connect you to a wide variety of organizations catering to the entire LGBTQ community. Then we only had Cher. And thank fucking God she was up to the challenge. The lighthouse beacon safely guiding a generation of men to the shore (which we would then turn into a gay beach).

She was our pride parade, our GLAAD, our *Out* magazine, our Trevor Project, all rolled into one. It is a debt that is impossible to repay. Although, I'd like to think after so many concerts and films and albums I've played at least some small part in keeping her filthy rich over the decades (and yes, I know there were some lean years). It is the very least every gay man can do.

It would be years before I would actually see a gay character on TV. And then it was only on special episodes where you usually had to hear "both sides of the issue" so someone still basically said "Yeah, but it's gross." Billy Crystal as Jodie on *Soap* was the first gay character I remember seeing as an actual series regular. He was smart and funny and sensitive but also wore dresses, which kind of prevented anyone from taking him too seriously. And he wasn't that different from all the other representations of gay men I had seen up until that point.

Everything changed, though, when I turned fourteen and *Dynasty* premiered. For those of you who don't know, *Dynasty* was a sensation that took over the fucking country for a few years in the '80s. It was our *Game of Thrones*, but with shoulder pads. I think I had my first orgasm when Linda Evans slapped Joan Collins across the face and called her a bitch. The two of them then rolling around the floor, ripping their clothes apart, and throwing vases at each other. The Golden Age of television.

But it was Steven Carrington, Blake Carrington's wayward son, who I really cared about. Steven Carrington was gay. And he was fucking hot. Tousled blond hair, pouty lips, athletic body, wealthy, and unapologetic. I had never seen a gay man like him before. This was even better than Cher. For the first time I wasn't alone. I had Steven Carrington. As played by Al Corley he was my dream man. Instantly he became "my type." He still is. You can't shake that shit. I learned in later years to diversify my portfolio, but it always comes back to Steven Carrington. Not Jack Coleman, though, who replaced Al Corley a few seasons later after he left the show. He was always the imposter Steven in my mind. Handsome in a bland way with none of the smoldering sexuality of a young Al Corley. No thank you, Jack Coleman, I'm not buying what you're selling. Steven Carrington will always only be Al Corley. Watch the scene on YouTube when he comes out to his father, Blake Carrington, played by John Forsythe. (Also the voice of Charlie on *Charlie's Angels*. What couldn't he do?) It is in the first episode of the series. And fourteen-year-old Gary is watching this alone in his basement. It was as if God himself had beamed it into our home. A hand from the heavens reaching out through the TV letting me know that there were others out there. And they looked like Steven Carrington.

I don't want to mislead you into thinking *Dynasty* was some kind of progressive series that created a positive image of gay life. Far from it. Blake Carrington ends up disowning Steven and accidentally killing his lover, Ted Dinard. (Who was not very attractive, so I was not very upset. "He could do so much better," I thought. "He could have *anyone!*") In later years Steven would become bisexual, then straight for a bit, then gay again. Marrying at one point Krystle's niece, Sammy Jo, as played to perfection by Heather Locklear.

But it was still the most major thing to happen in my life up until that point. If they were showing this on TV, how many of us must there actually be I wondered. A fucking lot. I was now connected to an invisible network that stretched from Queens all the way across the country. Like-minded young men sitting in front of their TV screens watching Al Corley (*not* Jack Coleman!) as Steven Carrington stand up to his domineering father and proclaim his love for another man (who, as I've already mentioned, would soon be killed, but whatever) with all of us silently cheering him on from deep within the recesses of our own private closets.

I'll be there soon, Steven. Wait for me.

PARAMOUNT PART II

I've been working at the Paramount Hotel for over two years. The last year as a bellman. What started out as a fun, sexy "survival" job was morphing into my actual job. Which was a lot less fun and sexy. At twenty-eight I was no longer the ingénue, thirty was now within spitting distance. Some of my fellow bellmen had already reached this milestone and were carrying other people's luggage well into their thirties. Wesley was thirty-six, and he stood out to me as a cautionary tale. "What's going to happen to him?" I couldn't help wonder every time we were on shift together. A struggling actor and model, he was still waiting for his big break. "He's almost *forty*!" A word I spit out the way you would rapist or pedophile. Of course it wasn't Wesley's future I was actually concerned about but my own. A budding writer who hasn't written, a budding actor who hasn't acted, I didn't do it all! I was planning to, though. Preparing myself with "life experience" for a novel that I would soon write. Very soon. I was just getting warmed up. My twenties merely a vocal exercise before the performance of my thirties. Foreplay for my real life, I convinced myself. Any moments of clarity ("I need to make some serious changes!") were quickly squashed and replaced with: "It's fine, I'm on my own schedule, everything's going to happen the way it should, things will work out, when I'm ready the universe will take care of it." And just underneath that, its twin voice whispering: "Why not *you*? Why hasn't it happened for *you* yet? Why is it easier for everyone else? It's not fair!!"

During this time, I'm working the overnight shift four days a week. I'm off the other three. More time to not write. I live in a sixth-floor walk-up on Christopher Street in a rent-controlled apartment. The kind of tenement building that you usually see in movies about Italian immigrants or the Triangle Shirtwaist Factory fire. Walking my bicycle up and down the six flights of stairs to ride to and from the hotel. In my early twenties I work as a bicycle teen-tour leader for American Youth Hostels, an organization that has long since gone out of business, probably because they had people as unqualified as myself leading their tours. (Two of the kids on my trips were hit by cars, not my fault, but I'll admit it makes me look unlucky at best.) I still enjoy riding my bike, though, and it is my main method of transportation as I race around Manhattan without a helmet, weaving in and out of traffic the way you do when

you're young and don't realize will die. A straight shot up Eighth
Avenue brings me to the hotel on Forty-sixth Street. It's summer and I arrive each night in a tank top and shorts, long '90s
hair, and I would carry my bike into the basement of the hotel,
where I would then change into my uniform.

And each night I would tell myself that I would not fall
asleep during my shift. I would stay awake, alert, dignified.
I would drink coffee from room service and usually be okay
the first few hours. By midnight all the other bellmen's shifts
had ended and it would just be me until 7:00 A.M. when my
relief came in. But by 3:00 A.M. I would inevitably fall asleep
behind the front desk on the dirty carpet. Drooling and snor-
ing all dignity long gone. When a guest needed something Lola
would nudge me with her foot. Lola was the one other person
who worked with me overnight. She had been working the
front desk at the hotel for years, long before it had been taken
over by Studio 54's Ian Schrager and transformed into one of
the first boutique hotels in the city. She was no-nonsense,
moved in slow motion, would hang up the phone on guests,
and I fucking loved her. Once housekeeping would close for
the evening they would roll up a cart of videos (guests rented
VHS videos then, it was a backward time, so much mortifies
me to write), and if guests wanted to rent a movie after midnight they would need to call the front desk and order it from
Lola and then I would bring it up. And 99.9 percent of rentals
at this time of night would be porn. All the movies on the list
had a number that corresponded to the title, so when ordering

you could just discreetly ask for number 215, saving yourself the humiliation. Except we liked to torture the guests, and Lola would make each of them say the title of the film out loud, nonsensically telling them this was because the computers were down overnight. (This was a '90s thing you could say and people would just respond "Oh, right.") Then Lola would repeat the title back to them. "Yes, we do have Edward Penishands available. I'll have the bellman bring Edward Penishands right up." It was as entertaining as it sounds. I knew if I was bringing up straight porn they'd open the door a crack and take the movie, and I knew if it was gay porn I was going to have to turn down an invitation to watch it, too, or worse. In the middle of the night people become animals. Just eating and fucking. Nothing fazed me, though, I'd seen it all. If somebody answered the door with clothes on, I considered it a bonus. Most of the gay guys were closeted married businessmen, you'd think it was the '50s. Sometimes I'd get a second call to return to the same room and I'd refuse to go up. I'd tell Lola to say I was with another guest. Or she'd just hang up on them. This went on every night. It would never have occurred to me to tell anyone that a guest had done or said something inappropriate. Because it happened all the time to everyone. It was just part of the job. When you didn't get propositioned was the time to worry.

The way I made most of my money on the overnight shift was from what I learned from the bellman who trained me. Terrence worked the night shift for years and I took over for him. He had a whole system in place to make money on what would normally be the least lucrative shift. We became friendly and he took me under his wing, showing me the ropes. Room service stopped at midnight, so if guests wanted anything they would have to order it from the bellman, who would then go out into Times Square to procure it. If a guest wanted, say, a turkey sandwich we would then go to the Korean deli and get one for three dollars and charge them fifteen. And they had to pay cash. We would tell them that up front. Same computers-being-down excuse. Again, the '90s. They would usually give you a twenty-dollar bill and tell you to keep the rest, so that's a seventeen-dollar profit for one sandwich. Not bad. And we could pretty much get anything in Times Square and mark it up. In making up the prices the trick was not to go too high so that a guest would question us, possibly letting management in on the scheme. Terrence knew all the hookers in Times Square, too, and introduced me to all of them when he took me on rounds one night, showing me where to get everything. It wasn't long before I'd be walking to the McDonald's on Broadway at 3:00 A.M. to get fries for a guest (eight dollars) and saying "hi" to at least half a dozen of them along the way. (Around this time I went to the theater with my mother, and after the show as we were walking along Eighth Avenue a hooker I knew said "Hi, Gary, how's it going?" and my mother was like "How do you know her?" "Oh. She's just a friend.")

One night I was late for work, it was pouring rain, so I took the subway. And when I got out of the station I started running for the hotel. I was wearing an outfit I got at Emporio Armani, which was the height of fashion then. I had charged this outfit to one of the credit cards that came in the mail that I would then use to buy clothes and groceries. I thought I looked so cute. It was shorts and a button-down shirt with sandals. All very summery and blousy and expensive. As I was running across Forty-sixth Street I slipped and fell in the street, hard, a taxi screeching to a stop to avoid hitting me. Tourists coming over from *Les Miz*, which had just emptied out, to see if I was okay. Yes, yes, I was fine, I said embarrassed. Hopping up and rushing into the lobby. One of the managers sees me. "What happened to you?" And I notice my leg is bleeding and my shorts are ripped, my shirt torn, and I'm filthy. And she takes me in the back to help clean me off and I'm laughing, not wanting to make a big thing of it. And as she opens the emergency kit and wipes the dirt off my knee I start crying. Suddenly I feel so stupid. These clothes I can't afford, ruined. Serves me right, I think. And I'm bleeding and wet and tired and I still have to stay up all night and I don't know what I'm doing.

But I go on working at the hotel. It's so easy to push something back down once it bubbles up. I have a boyfriend, I'm still young, I go out, I see shows, I'm busy. And summer goes by.

Before it was taken over by Ian Shrager, the Paramount was also a residential hotel, and dozens of permanent residents lived there. After he bought it, Ian payed them all off and they moved out. All except two. Ellen and Mr. Rosen. He couldn't pay either of them enough to leave, they had nowhere else to go. This had been their home for decades. So they continued living at the hotel once it was turned into the trendiest spot in Manhattan. Ellen was in her seventies and limped and was unkempt, always in the same disturbingly flimsy housedress. She spent most of her days in the lobby making disgusted faces at the guests, but she loved all the bellmen. We got her breakfast and picked up her medications and looked after her. She was a real piece of work. Loud and opinionated and nasty, she could also be unexpectedly kind. Mr. Rosen was in his eighties and very dapper and polite and quiet. Her complete opposite. And they despised each other. I don't know why, some long-simmering feud that predated any of us. They would both spend the day at opposite ends of the dimly lit Philippe Starck–designed lobby, shooting occasional filthy looks at each other. You'd think since neither of them had anyone else in their lives they would have formed some sort of friendship at this point. Instead they behaved as if they were the heads of two warring families out of Shakespeare. You couldn't help get sucked in. "What's he doing?" she'd say to us, nodding toward him. "Just reading the paper." Then she'd make a noise as if that was the most vile thing anyone could possibly do. Ellen rarely left the hotel, but when she did it was impossible to distinguish her from a homeless woman. Outside of her familiar environment she was disoriented and mean, often talking to herself and yelling at tourists on their way to *Les Miz*. (*Les Miz* played across the street from the hotel for my entire time there. On Wednesday matinee days buses of high school students would pull up outside the theater and the girls would all giggle and shriek at whatever cute doorman was working that day. Sometimes, when I needed a lift, I would position myself outside the hotel just as the girls were coming off the buses and wave as they pointed and giggled at me. It felt way more fucking good than it should have.) When any of us would see Ellen outside of the hotel we would steer her back. She recognized our uniforms and would gladly come with us, complaining about what had happened to New York along the way. She couldn't remember our names, we were all sweetheart to her.

Ellen was up early in the morning. When I'd see her limping off the elevator, I knew my shift was almost ended. I'd get her a coffee and one for me, too. And she'd ask how the night was and we would bitch about people who worked there, people she didn't like, the guests. She complained constantly and loudly about everything. Most of the women she referred to as sluts and the boys were all her favorites. Her face shedding forty years when she would coquettishly say good morning to Michael, the best-looking bellman, who was also a model. Michael was so good-looking I was afraid to talk to him. Giggling like one of the schoolgirls going to a matinee of *Les Miz* every time he walked by.

"Can you cover my shift tomorrow, I have a photo shoot," he says to me one day.

"Oh, my God, yeah, of course, no, I'm not doing anything, sure, a photo shoot for what?"

"An underwear campaign for Calvin Klein."

I must've blacked out right then and there because I don't remember anything after that. I think that was the last time I saw him. A month later there was an enormous billboard of him in white briefs looming over Times Square. Life could be so cruel. Even Michael had somehow figured it out. Why couldn't I? Granted, he looked like he was carved from stone, but still, it wasn't fair. He was the person who got out and I was the person left behind to point at underwear boxes saying, "I know him."

It is the end of summer and I am working the overnight shift with Lola. I fall asleep as usual around 3:00 A.M. on the filthy carpet behind the front desk. It is a quiet night. There are no sandwiches to get, no trips to McDonald's, nobody even calls for a video. I make little to no money. Lola nudges me with her foot around 6:00 A.M. Guests are checking out, she tells me. I bring a cart with me up to their room. It is two women from Spain both elegantly dressed. They have several suitcases each and need a taxi to JFK. I lay on the charm. "How was your trip? Did you see any shows?" etc. I pile their four suitcases onto the cart and deliver them to the lobby where they wait while I get them a taxi and load their bags. I tell the driver "JFK," the women then come out, and I hold the door open for them wishing them a safe trip, chatting long enough to give one of them time to go into her purse and fish for some money. But, no, nothing. They both say thank you and get in the car and

that's it. I close the door after them and then something inside me snaps. As the taxi pulls away I slam on the trunk twice
with my open palm. "Hey!" The driver stops and I walk to the
passenger side where the confused woman looks at me. She
opens the window. "It's customary in this country to tip!" I say.
I'm angry. She nervously reaches into her purse, takes out a
twenty-dollar bill and holds it out to me. I take it and the taxi
pulls away. I stand there for a minute, stunned. Ashamed. I
walk back into the lobby, where Ellen is now sitting. She looks
at me. "Are you okay, sweetheart?" "I'm fine," I say and get us
each a cup of coffee.

I quit a few weeks later and shortly after that move to LA. I
start writing. I never stop.

CAFÉ SHA SHA

I'm forty-eight. My boyfriend and I go to Mykonos on vacation. We had met there over a dozen years before. I saw him walk by while I was eating dinner in a taverna and started talking to him. We spent the week together. I was young, in the best shape of my life, with thick dark hair. None of which still apply. Brad was twenty-three and blond-ish and handsome.

On the surface it appears that Mykonos is the most carefree destination in the world, where you do whatever you want whenever you want, but the truth is your days are dictated with an almost military precision, each one scheduled practically to the minute. You wake up at noon and have breakfast. You head to the beach around 2:00 P.M., *not before*. Lunch is at the beach around 4:00. You leave the beach at 6:30. Then you walk around town, get a frappé, and decide where to go for sunset.

After you watch the sunset you go back to your hotel. You get ready for dinner, have a cocktail, then walk around town again. Dinner is at 11:00 P.M., not before. After dinner you make your way to the gay bar (then Pierro's, now Jackie O's). You arrive at 1:00 A.M. Again, not before. You stand outside the bar. Seeing who is there. Whispering to your friends. And then an hour later you go inside. You drink and you dance. You stay out till 4:00 or 5:00. You wake up at noon and repeat. You do not veer from this schedule. Nobody tells it to you. Nobody has to. You just automatically begin doing it. (You don't even realize you're on a schedule.) Day after day it repeats. You start to recognize people. You make friends. You sit with them at the beach, you join them at dinner, dance with them at the bars. And then a new group of people starts arriving and you recognize fewer and fewer of them. And you realize your time there is coming to an end and the island now belongs to this new group of gay men from England, and Sweden, and Italy and Canada and the States until the next group of men arrives to gradually replace them, and the next, and this will go on and on, year after year, long after you have left the island.

But that first week Brad and I meet is perfect. Every minute I want to stretch to a month. We go out each night, late dinner, dancing. We know all the boys. We flirt with them, we dance with them. A squeeze of the arm, a pat on the butt, a grab of a pec. Smiles, winks, all of us members of the same little club.

Brad and I return to Greece several times over the years. The week always plays out the same. But never with the in-

tensity of our first time there. It's been a while since we've returned, and now here we are again. Back on the island, back
out dancing, in a room packed full of men. But something is
different this time. I notice it, then brush it away. And then no
longer able to chalk it up to a freak occurrence, I'm forced to
admit to myself what has happened. I am no longer a member
of the private little club. I am no longer an object of desire.
I have become almost invisible to these men, men who had
been my compadres, my partners in crime, my brothers. I go
up to the bar and no one grabs me. I make my way through the
crowded room and no one pushes against me. No one gropes
me inappropriately, no one is making eye contact with me. The
party is going on, but I am no longer a part of it. It is a private
club of younger men speaking their younger language. I am
now just a body preventing them from getting to the body they
want. My membership revoked. I am in a new country. I have
been banished. And then I realize, of course, when I was going
out all those years, I was not flirting with forty-eight-year-
olds. I don't even remember *seeing* any of them, so it kind of
makes perfect sense. Here I was, now on the other side of it.
But no one had prepared me. No one told me it was happening *tonight*. And I look at Brad on the dance floor. Still young
enough, still in the thick of it. They all smile at him, maneu-
ver to dance with him, flirt. He is still one of the stars of the
show while I am being shown the exit. Trying to linger as long
as I can but being pushed to the door. I have had a good run,
I can't deny that. Who knew I would miss with such an ache

having my ass grabbed by drunken men as I made my way to the bathroom?

Brad and I make eye contact from across the room. He motions for me to join him on the dance floor. I decline, I make a gesture that implies "You dance, I'll be over here." He smiles back "Got it" and continues dancing with all the other young men around him. One giant throbbing mass that I am just on the outside of. He has no idea that my life has ended this night. I feel someone's eyes on me, I turn. It is a man over fifty, he gives me a sympathetic smile. "What are you lookin' at, Grandpa?!"

I remember the first time finding out I was attractive to other men. My sister Maria was starting college at NYU. She needs a part-time job, so I go with her into the city one after- noon to look for one. I'm sixteen, she's eighteen, and it's 1982. We walk through Greenwich Village together, going into ran- dom cafés and restaurants. She is looking for a waitress job for after classes. She doesn't have any experience, her last job being at our local McDonald's. We go into a dozen restau- rants with no luck. Then I spot a place on Hudson, just off Christopher Street. "Try here," I say. The place is called Café Sha Sha and I love the look of it. Like something you would see while strolling in Europe. (I end up living around the block from it a few years later when I am working as a bellman at the Paramount Hotel.) She goes in while I wait outside. And peering through the window I see all these beautiful men, waiters preparing for their shift. In T-shirts, laughing, tying aprons around their slim waists, sleeves rolled up revealing biceps. This was the West Village in the early '80s and it was the center of the gay universe. I could feel my heart beating as I waited for her to come out. And when she did: "I got the job!" They hire her on the spot. "I told you," I say, "I had a feeling about that place," and we take the subway back to Queens.

Maria commutes to NYU from home. On nights when she works late at the café my dad drives into the city to pick her up. (My parents were unusually generous with driving us places. For years, my mother on her day off from work would drive my sister into the city Saturdays while she studied at the Manhattan School of Music. Sitting there all day reading her book while Maria took classes. My dad driving us every day during the summers to a pool on Long Island. Then most nights to Carvel for ice cream. I won't even pick them up at the airport when they visit. But I send a nice car.) Sometimes I go with him to pick her up. Driving over the Williamsburg Bridge at 2:00 A.M. I get a thrill. (Things stayed open late then.) On these nights, I go into the café to get her while my father is parked outside. Usually, she will just be finishing up. I loved when I had to wait for her a few minutes. I would stand shyly and watch the men finishing their work, joking with one another and they would all say "Hi." And I just stood there, head bowed, eyes downcast like a geisha. Nodding politely. So afraid was I of saying anything wrong. These men all perfect. The oldest no more than twenty-three. Just those few minutes waiting for her was a glimpse into a secret society that I knew

I would be joining soon. (I could wait. I had already spent so many years of my life waiting. Patiently. It's why I can sit in the theater for three hours of *King Lear* without even blinking.)

My sister, soon after she starts working there, tells me all these men are gay. All except one. His name was Craig, and he was perhaps the best-looking of all. He was an aspiring actor. Never was my sister more fabulous than when she was talking to Craig or simply clearing a table with him. I would've killed someone to pick up dirty glasses with Craig.

One night Maria and I are watching TV in our basement and during a commercial break she casually says something that sends me spinning for years.

"The guys at the café said you're going to be very popular."

My heart stops. "What does that mean?" I ask. But I know exactly what it means.

"I don't know, they just said 'your brother's going to be very popular.'"

She leaves it at that. (But I still think about it now, almost forty years later.) They talk about me?? This is more than I could have possibly hoped for. They noticed me, they talked about me, and they liked what they saw. I could be one of them when I am a little older. Travel among them. Laugh with them, work with them, go out with them. Kiss them. It was too much to take in. I acted as if it didn't mean that much to me. That I thought it was weird, in fact, that they had even mentioned me. But something started that day. I felt seen for the first time.

And these men, boys really, were letting me know that it was going to be okay. In fact, better than okay. I was going to be popular. A word that had never been used to describe me before. And now here it was being used by the people I would want most to see me that way. I could wait. It would just be a few more years. (And then I would recognize one or two or more of them out in the clubs or the bars or on the street and I would tell them my story and how we had met years ago. "You made it!" they would say, remembering. "Yes," I would say, "I made it.")

These little trips into the city to Café Sha Sha to get my sister at the end of her shifts were the little sips of water I needed to keep me going. To get to glance at these men. Smile shyly at them. And they were so friendly and kind to me and everything seemed so easy for them. The way they talked, the way they moved, the way they interacted. I wanted to ask my sister everything about them. What were their likes, their dislikes, did they say anything about me today?? Desperate for any scrap of information. But I couldn't. "How was work?" was all I could manage.

Then one day, she tells me something incredible. Craig, the straight waiter, auditioned for the role of Steven Carrington on *Dynasty*. It is down to him and one other actor, and they are flying him out to Los Angeles to meet with the producers. Al Corley, who created the role, will be leaving the show. (His handsome face blown off in an oil rig explosion on the season-ending cliffhanger.) To think that I would know the actor playing Steven Carrington! It's all almost too much. Things were moving so quickly! (And not at all. Nothing was actually happening to me.) The days where Craig was waiting to find out if he got the role dragged by. I would go to sleep thinking, "Maybe we'll hear tomorrow."

"Has he heard anything?" I'd ask Maria after she got home from every shift.

"What? Oh, that, I don't know," she replies.

This was barely on her radar and yet it consumed my every waking moment. "WELL ASK HIM!" When he doesn't get the part the disappointment I feel is like a rock in my stomach. To have us come so close and then to have it yanked away . . . I have literally spoken to Craig maybe once up until this point but I feel like what has happened has happened to both of us. What I think this would have meant for me had he gotten the part is unclear. But the thought that I could be adjacent, even in the most tangential way, to someone's rise to fame—well, the excitement was almost too much to bear. How did this end up being my life? Well, it was technically *Craig's* life, but still. . . .

After I get over the disappointment of Craig not getting the part of Steven Carrington I find out from my sister he is now up for a part on *One Life to Live*, my favorite soap opera. It was as if Craig were rattling around in my brain, picking off my obsessions one by one, or that I was controlling him with my mind, sending him out into the world to do my bidding. If these things were happening to me, they couldn't have been any more thrilling.

He gets the part. To think that I live in a world where you could be waiting tables one day and the next be Llanview's new leading man. I celebrated in my head for both of us. "YES! WE GOT IT!" A short time later I would see him on the show playing Cassie's new boyfriend. Cassie was Dorian Lord's daughter and thereby an important character, so this was very good for us. It was no Steven Carrington, but then again what was?

What if my sister and I had not walked into Café Sha Sha that day? How different my life would be.

Maria loses touch with Craig. (He doesn't stay on the show very long. Instead he becomes the star of a new nighttime soap opera that lasts for only a few episodes and then goes on to star in a horror film titled *Nightbreed* (also starring Anne Bobby, an actress I studied with at Oxford University the summer I was nineteen and whose ill-fated Broadway musical *Smile* I go to see her in the following year) before going on to eventually star in *A River Runs Through It* with Brad Pitt. We did well, Craig and I.) And soon after that Maria stops working at the café. My visits now to see these men abruptly ended. And then I am seventeen and then I am eighteen and then I am nineteen.

And maybe it is around this time, and maybe it is a little later. But Maria tells me these men she had worked with had died. She has found this out recently. Bumping into someone who used to work there with her. Or she stops by the café again and finds out that way. I can't remember how it happens. I remember she is upset when she tells me. I don't ask a lot of questions. But they have all died or are dying. It is around 1984, '85. And it seems impossible to believe. These were the men who were going to welcome me. Who I was going to bump into in clubs and bars, on the street. And they were gone.

At the time I thought all these men dying were so much older than I was. It was so far from me, it felt. Another world. Only years later did I realize we were a breath apart.

I move into the city after college when I'm twenty-two. Such a short amount of time later from when I first walked into Café Sha Sha. And in that time, while I was waiting, a generation of gay men vanish. And no one really says that much about it. No one seems that upset. We are disposable, like tissues. These men who had reached a hand out to me when I needed it most. Had shown me kindness. Had let me know it was going to be okay. Sometimes I imagine I'm sixteen and I'm standing in the back of Café Sha Sha waiting for my sister again and I'm watching these men, men whose names I have long since forgotten and perhaps never known, men who I have only ever seen a handful of times over thirty-five years ago but still see clearly. And they are young and beautiful and this time I don't stand shyly in the corner, scared, nervous, insecure, I walk confidently up to them, I smile, I reach out and I say thank you.

I *was* popular, and I had boyfriends, and I had one-night stands, and flirted and I was flirted with, was groped and grabbed and kissed, and this goes on for years and I meet Brad and we are together and more years go by and suddenly I'm forty-eight and standing in this club in Mykonos on this night and I look around this room full of impossibly young men, like so many rooms I have stood in before it, and I move through the crowd. I find Brad. And I dance. Because I can.

I'D REALLY LIKE TO THANK

My sister Maria Abeshouse, and my brother-in-law Adam Abeshouse, for always supporting me, especially at a time when I needed it most.

Julia Markus, my creative writing professor at Hofstra University, for teaching me that I had a voice, and giving me the confidence to (eventually) use it.

My dear friend Jeffrey Richman, for introducing me to Patti LuPone so that that story could finally have an ending. (And forty years later, I still stand by there can be no understudy for Patti LuPone.)

My assistant (and friend) Tom McDonald, for reading early drafts of these essays and (usually) saying what I wanted to hear.

My agents Jay Sures and Albert Lee at UTA. The best.

Tony Peyrot for his years of guidance and friendship.

The lovely and talented Alasdair McLellan, for his photo of me for this book jacket. I felt like a model (finally).

At Flatiron Books, Amy Einhorn and Bob Miller, for giving me the opportunity to write this book. And for your faith in it once it was written. Thank you.

Also at Flatiron Books, Marlena Bittner, Emily Walters, Jeremy Pink, Nancy Trypuc, Katherine Turro, and Cristina Gilbert. Thanks, guys!

James Melia, my editor, and now friend (the LAST one I'm going to make), for believing in this book (and me), and for being such a delight to work with. (Definitely *not* a shitty millennial.)

Brad, for being even better than Steven Carrington.

And Mom and Dad, for everything.

ABOUT THE AUTHOR

Gary Janetti is a writer and producer of such shows as *Family Guy, Will & Grace*, and *Vicious*. He lives in Los Angeles.